TRUST GOD
He Really Does Love You

A Revolutionary Book About God The Father

by Dr. Jerry Robeson

Published by Shiloh Publishing House
P.O. Box 100
Woodburn, OR 97071-3631

First Edition, 1996

TRUST GOD
He Really Does Love You

It is recommended that the reader also read Jerry and Carol's two previous books on spiritual warfare which have become the definitive texts on the subject.

Other Books:
STRONGMAN'S HIS NAME WHAT'S HIS GAME
STRONGMAN'S HIS NAME II

A catalog and order blank can be found in the back of this book showing the Robeson's other books and teaching tapes, both audio and video, which will be of benefit in your spiritual life.

Shiloh Publishing House
P.O. Box 100
Woodburn, OR 97071-3631

TABLE OF CONTENTS

TABLE OF ILLUSTRATIONS

PREFACE

While writing our book, **Strongman's His Name What's His Game**, it became apparent to Carol and I that it would require that we clearly differentiate between Godly and satanic actions if we had any hope of correctly presenting the spiritual warfare teaching God had revealed to us. How could the people who read our books and attended our seminars apply our teaching to their problems if they didn't know who was actually causing them? If the problems were initiated because God was testing them in some way, then they should cooperate with God. But if it was an action of Satan, they had the right and authority as a child of God to stop what the enemy was trying to accomplish in their life and win the battle according to the Promises of God's Word.

We observed also that the spiritual warfare battlefield was littered with unnecessary casualties because many of the combatants were "shooting" at each other or at God instead of saving their spiritual "bullets" for the actual enemy, Satan. Two major areas were causing this situation:

(1) A lack of sound, biblical teaching of spiritual warfare principles; many people just made things up as they went along, creating a situational, experiential theology that was off the wall. (2) Many Christians were listening to and acting upon satanic deception without understanding that it was from Satan. Then to further exacerbate the error because of the deception they were experiencing, they had a tendency to reject the counsel of anyone who attempted to point out what God's Word had to say about it.

We could not begin to tell you how many burned-out people we encountered who practiced that particular brand of spiritual warfare activity. The horror stories of what happened under those circumstances were incredible. Many lost out completely with God. Others rejected the whole concept of spiritual warfare because it had messed up their lives in one way or the other. "I tried that," they would say, "and it didn't work so I just stay away from that kind of thing now." Some are still trying to make it work, which will only create additional horror stories in the future.

How tragic that a viable part of God's Word is in danger of being nullified because God's people cannot recognize the deception of Satan and expose his devices. Many leaders look at this scene and chose the path of least resistance by encouraging their people to steer clear of spiritual warfare in general. But Jesus and Paul spent a large part of the New Testament instructing Christians on how to maintain the victory in their lives that Jesus Christ won over Satan and accomplish God's Will for reaching this world with the Gospel. That cannot happen if Satan is running wild, doing anything he wants to do, without any confrontational, biblical action from the Body of Christ.

As we looked at all of this, it was a temptation to tip toe past the whole subject of authenticating what Godly actions are. Why shake the hornet's nest and risk the wrath and revulsion of Christendom in general? Why challenge the many incorrect traditions, theories and unbiblical ideas about what God does and doesn't do? I grew up in the church so I've heard them all, usually expressed by people with loud voices, red faces and with their veins standing out on their necks.

But the easy way usually ends up being the hard way so we decided to emphasize from the beginning that God does good things and Satan is the one who does evil things. And of course there is the third ingredient—that which we do to ourselves—which must be taken into consideration.

When it came time to write my doctoral dissertation, it presented an appropriate time to research the subject and come up with a scripturally- balanced character analysis of God that would hopefully dissipate the oppressive cloud of confusion and deception which stifles the healthy relationship God longs to have with His children. That will also be the goal of this book.

It is my heartfelt desire that this information will be of help to you in your walk with God.

TRUST GOD HE REALLY DOES LOVE YOU

CHAPTER ONE

A woman in the audience began verbally attacking me in a disjointed manner as soon as I started teaching the first session of one of our "Strongman's His Name" seminars. I could tell by her slurred speech that she was not totally responsible for her actions and I expected to see an usher come to my rescue to handle the situation. But nobody moved a muscle. In retrospect, I suppose they were waiting to see what I would do with this obviously troubled woman because, after all, this was a spiritual warfare seminar my wife, Carol, and I were conducting.

In the fleeting seconds I had to decide what action I should take, two thoughts flashed through my consciousness: (1) You're on your own, buddy, humanly speaking, and, (2) This woman is only disturbed, not demon possessed. So I moved the microphone closer to my mouth and kept on teaching as though the woman was not there. For what seemed like an eternity we had a pro and con presentation of the seminar.

I was teaching about God's Character and how to recognize Godly actions in our lives. As I progressed through the explanation I noticed that the woman's comments became fewer in number until finally my voice was the only one speaking in the auditorium.

On the way to the motel after the service, Carol told me what our vocal audience member had shared with her after the service. She had recently lost her nine-year-old son in a tragic accident during a family outing. The boy had gotten too close to a fast-moving stream cascading over the edge of a high cliff. Suddenly the ground had caved in under his feet and he was thrown into the raging water and swept over the precipice to his death.

The accident was tragic enough, but what caused her additional, needless pain was the fact that Christians, in an attempt to comfort her, had told her it was God who had taken her boy. Unfortunately this is not an isolated incident. I, too, have heard people make such statements over the years. Their desire is to comfort the bereaved, but in so doing they actually create a larger problem. These people tell the grief-stricken person in hushed tones, "God works in mysterious ways, His wonders to perform," or "God takes the one you love the most," or "The closer you get to God, the more He tests you," or "We can't question the Sovereign actions of God."

The problem with this kind of grief counseling is that it had pushed this lady to the edge of a nervous breakdown; she was on tranquilizers and nearly out of control.

When I had begun teaching about God's Character, she figured I was going to follow the same line of reasoning she had been told concerning her boy's death. In her drug-induced state she wanted to warn the congregation that this was not something God does to people. But after listening to me, in between her outbursts, she realized that I was not taking the direction she had anticipated and settled down to listen to the remainder of the session.

She told Carol that she could accept the fact that Satan would do such a treacherous, evil thing to her because she and her husband had been living in a backslidden state when the accident occurred. But she just could not believe that God was capable of doing something so cruel to her son and to her family.

When she finally realized from the seminar teaching that God was not the One who had caused her boy's death, the conflict was resolved, she stopped taking the tranquilizers and was back to normal in a matter of three days!

"A God Who Kills Babies"

Another parent expressed his feelings for God after the death of his two-year-old son, "...the death of my son created a hatred for God where before I'd felt only apathy. I didn't want anything to do with a God who killed babies. In fact, I figured I'd rather go to hell to be with the devil than go to heaven and be with a baby-killing God."[1]

When he learned about God's true character, he accepted Christ as His Savior and once again the conflict was resolved.

The Ted Turner Tragedy

On the other hand, the sad results in the life of cable TV magnate, Ted Turner, illustrates how dangerous the fallout can be from a faulty knowledge of what Godly actions truly are. He told of his reaction to a death in his family many years ago when delivering his acceptance speech after being named "Humanist of the Year" by the American Humanist Association.

"Turner explained how he was raised in an 'extremely religious' environment, including six years at a Christian prep school, Bible Training, daily chapel services and regular meetings with evangelists.

"'With no other influences in my life at the time—and the way it was pounded into us so much—I think I was saved seven or eight times,' Turner joked.

"The young Turner actually even considered missionary work. But then, his younger sister got ill. Ted says he prayed and prayed. Five long, painful years later, she died.

"'I couldn't understand why this loving God that I had been taught about so long would allow someone to suffer so—someone small and someone who hadn't done anything wrong.' he told the humanists. 'I prayed and nothing happened, of course.'

"'I thought about it and said to myself, I'm not sure if I want any part of this,' he recalled. 'If God is love, and He is all powerful, why does He allow these things to happen. This interpretation that it's just His will—I just can't get enthusiastic about that. I began to lose my faith and the more I lost, the better I felt.'"[2]

Think of how different his life could have been and how much he could have accomplished for God with the abilities he possesses in the area of cable television, if he had received correct teaching concerning God and His Character.

Because of this satanicly-inspired character assassination of God, it is an accepted part of the grieving process to blame God for the loss of a loved one. For instance, "It is common to be angry at God..." after suffering a miscarriage.[3]

Insurance companies call hurricanes, tornadoes, earthquakes, floods and similar disasters, "Acts of God."

Some parents threaten their children with the fact that God will "get them" or do something bad to them if they continue their disobedience.

Is it any mystery that sinners think it is better to maintain their distance from a God they believe is cruel and vicious and whose supposed delight is to irresponsibly punish the human race with terrible, destructive actions?

Some Christians Also Have Mistaken Ideas About God

Unfortunately, sinners are not the only ones who believe these things about God. Many Christians also believe the very worst about God for a variety of reasons:

(1) Their earthly father abused them physically or mentally while they were growing up. They reason that God the Father falls into the same category by virtue of His Fatherly relationship to His creation. As a result, all kinds of emotions flood through their minds and distort their thinking when the word "Father" is mentioned, making it very difficult for them to relate to a Father God relationship.

(2) Faulty religious doctrines and traditions which portray God as some kind of Clint Eastwood, "make my day" kind of cowboy, who periodically indulges in Saturday night binges of violence and killing to see if His children really love him or to teach them some lesson or to get the sinner's attention.

(3) Various occasions in the Bible seem to support the fact that God occasionally used and consequently still

uses fits of behavior, that can only be described as demonic, to bring about His "Godly" plans.

(4) Some believe God has a right to do whatever He wants to do to His creation because it is His creation to do with as He pleases. In fact, they believe it is absolutely necessary that He be brutal to cause certain types of people to respect and obey Him for fear of being annihilated if they do not.

(5) There are those who believe God does evil things because they would act in that manner if they had the opportunity and the total power that God possesses. They simply superimpose their own personality and thought patterns upon God.

(6) Others mistakenly place God in the same category as an earthly dictator who does whatever he feels like doing because he is a law unto himself.

(7) Some Christians apparently find it comforting to believe they have a secret weapon to use on people who disagree with them. For instance, they intimate in so many words, "If you aren't careful I'll turn God loose on you and people have been known to drop dead when I did this in the past!"

(8) Finally, there is a school of thought which tries to have it both ways. They say that sometimes God does good things and sometimes He does bad things. This ambivalent position causes teachers and pastors to swing from one extreme to the other according to the side of God they wish to emphasize, which further confuses people's thinking about God. When they want to show a loving God, they use the scriptures that support that side. If they want to frighten people into obeying God, they show the "violent" side of God that supposedly puts diseases on people, arranges car accidents and sends disasters of nature, among other deadly things.

The amazing fact is that there are scriptures in the Bible that seem to support all of the above mistaken, even libelous ideas, traditions and concepts of God. However, it must also be noted that the Bible can be used to prove nearly anything a given individual would like to prove if the scriptures are taken out of context and twisted sufficiently.

Describe God To Me

So what is God the Father really like? How would you accurately describe God the Father to someone who has never heard of Him or read a Bible, has no idea of who He is, what He does, how he/she should relate to Him, or what His motivation is in dealing with the human race.

Carrying the analogy one step further, this person would also know nothing about Satan; who he is, what he does, how he/she should relate to him, or what his motivation is in dealing with the human race.

The answer to the question would seem to be a simple matter of opening a Bible and showing the person what it has to say about God the Father and Satan. After all, their characters are established and set in concrete. God the Father says about Himself, "For I am the Lord, I change not;" (Malachi 3:6) Jesus, speaking of Himself as a member of the Godhead, says that He is, "...the same, yesterday, today and forever." (Hebrews 13:8) Based on that truth, if God is one thing today, He will be **exactly** the same a month, a year or even an eternity from now because He has no "good" or "bad" days, only "eternal sameness."

The Master Of Disguises

Satan is the variable in this problem of understanding what God does and does not do. Although his character was frozen in place after his rebellion against God as Lucifer, he nevertheless camouflages himself to appear as someone other than who he really is to deceive mankind into disobeying God's Laws.

Paul warns, "For such are false apostles, deceitful workers, transforming themselves into apostles of Christ. And no marvel; for Satan himself is transformed into an angel of light. Therefore it is no great thing if his ministers also be transformed as ministers of righteousness;" (2 Cor. 11:13-15)

For instance, Satan will deliberately appear God-like while making a pronouncement that is contrary to God's Word. Entire religious organizations have come into being because an angelic-like creature supposedly gave them a great "revelation" that does not agree with the truth of God's Word. Books have been written that were inspired by "beings of light." Even Christians have had a figure, bathed in tremendous light, tell them "truths" that do not agree with the Word of God. So just because light is involved in an experience does not necessarily mean it is Godly because Satan is a master of disguises.

He Did It!

Another favorite trick of Satan is to do something of a destructive nature and then point his finger at God, intimating that God was the One who caused it. The human race quickly adopted this trick when Eve blamed Adam for being deceived. Children blame their brothers or sisters for what they actually did. Husbands blame wives and vice versa. In fact, it seems that no one is to blame for anything anymore.

The bad part is that even after the truth has eventually been sorted out, the innocent party's reputation still suffers from having been associated with the evil action for even a short period of time. In like manner, God's Name has been discredited by all the satanic finger pointing.

This deceitfulness creates a smokescreen around Satan's actions that makes it extremely difficult at times to judge who is actually responsible for the evil deeds. Consequently, the line between satanic and Godly actions becomes blurred. The confusion generated by these satanic tricks creates doubt and fear in people's minds about God the Father, which in turn keeps them in a constant state of uncertainty about what God actually does and does not do to them. The end result is that people are hindered from entering into the healthy Father/son-daughter relationship God longingly desires to have with His children.

Returning to the original question and answer, it is not just a matter of opening a Bible and showing someone who God is. Many have done that and, because of Satan's insidious deception, have come up with a "monster" who is light years away from what God truly is.

What Then Can Be Done To Unveil God's True Character?

The Apostle Paul points out that truth can only be found in the Bible by those who correctly interpret the Word of God. "Study to show yourselves approved unto God, a workman that needeth not to be ashamed, rightly dividing the word of truth." (2 Tim. 2:15) There is a correct way and a wrong way to interpret Scripture and those who "...rightly divide the word of truth..." are rewarded with a clear view of God's revelation knowledge that is compatible with both Testaments of the Bible.

Although the Bible has been used incorrectly in the past to "prove" many erroneous assumptions about God, the bottom line of **who** God is and **what** He does **still** can be found **only** in His message to mankind, the Bible; correctly interpreted, and according to the laws of interpretation.

So let us look into the Word of God and find what Godly actions consist of and, as a matter of contrast because of the relentless deception of Satan, what are satanic actions. When this conflict is resolved correctly, it frees people to enter into a trusting, loving relationship with their Heavenly Father without hesitation or fear. They also learn to recognize and resist Satan's tricks and deceptions which results in a life of victory as a child of God.

CHAPTER TWO

The first step in unraveling the mystery of God's character or attributes is to observe very closely how Jesus, the Son of God, characterized His Father. "...no one fully knows and accurately understands the Son except the Father; and no one fully knows and accurately understands the Father except the Son and **anyone to whom the Son deliberately wills to make Him known**." (Matt. 11:27 Amplified Bible) (Author's emphasis)

According to James 1:17, every good thing that happens to any human being is the result of God's direct, personal intervention in their life. "Every good and every perfect gift is from above, and cometh down from the Father of lights, with whom is no variableness, neither shadow of turning." Anything truly good that happens in our life is not a matter of experiencing "good luck" **if** we understand that **100%** of every good thing that has ever taken place in our life has come **directly** from the hand of God.

Of course the "good" that takes place in our life must genuinely have a good affect on our life for it to be an act of God. Winning the sweepstakes is not necessarily good if it triggers a host of evil consequences, such as divorce, immorality, addictions to alcohol or drugs, gambling, loss of good friends or the addition of evil friends. In such cases, what was thought to have been good was actually the worst thing that could possibly have happened.

The case of Buddy Post illustrates the fact that winning the lottery can be a worst case scenario. "In 1988, he won $16.2 million in the Pennsylvania Lottery. Since then, he was convicted of assault, his sixth wife left him, his brother was convicted of trying to kill him and his landlady successfully sued him for one-third of the jackpot.

"The crumbling mansion he bought with his winnings is half-filled with paperwork from bankruptcy proceedings and lawsuits. The gas was shut off, and Post feels lucky to have electricity and a telephone."[1]

The good God does in our life **always** produces positive results.

A further indication of the meaning of James 1:17 concerns the fact that the Hebrew and Greek languages use no punctuation marks—no underlining, no exclamation points or quotation marks to indicate what the writers wanted to emphasize as being important in the Bible. Instead, they used repetition to signal what they considered to be significant truths, just as James did in this verse when he said, "..with whom is no variableness, neither shadow of turning." Both phrases mean virtually the same thing, which was how James put additional weight on the fact that God never,

ever changes.

The disciples had a problem with this concept that Jesus revealed about His Father. They saw Jesus forgive sins, heal the sick, deliver the demon possessed and raise the dead. He claimed to be the Son of God, but He didn't fit their Old Testament beliefs about God the Father.

The Pharisees believed the God of the Old Testament was a hard, cruel, vindictive Being who wiped out people and nations at a whim. If Jesus was the Son of God, why didn't He act like His Father? If He was indeed the Messiah as He claimed to be, why didn't He free the nation of Israel from the bondage of the Roman government? Why didn't He destroy the Romans?

They Missed The Forest For The Trees

In fact, it is probable that the major reason the Pharisees rejected Jesus as their Messiah and had Him crucified was because He claimed to be the Son of God, but did not match their profile of the God of the Old Testament. They accused Jesus of blasphemy when He declared, "I and my Father are one. Then the Jews took up stones again to stone him." (John 10:30,31) **And because the Pharisees misjudged God's character, they missed the Messiah and went to Hell!** "Ye serpents, ye generation of vipers, how can ye escape the damnation of hell?" (Matt. 23:33) Nothing could illustrate more clearly the reality that it is not a light thing to reject God and His actions because of prejudicial thinking.

One day Philip asked Jesus about this subject. "Lord, show us the Father and it sufficeth us." (John 10:8) Or, what is God the Father really like? That seemed to be a reasonable question, but Jesus was not happy with it. "Jesus saith unto him, have I been so long time with you, and yet hast thou not known me, Philip? He that hath seen me hath seen the Father." (v. 9) After all this time, Philip, you should have already figured out that the Father and I are exactly the same in our purpose, motivation and character.

This Shocked the Disciples

The disciples were undoubtedly astonished at the answer. Passages of scripture from the Old Testament probably flashed through their minds of a God of vengeance in action. The knew Jesus hadn't killed anyone. He hadn't put sickness on people to teach them something. He hadn't made anyone poor so they could learn humility. How could the God of the Old Testament and Jesus be exactly alike?

There are still those who have the same problem with the answer Jesus gave Philip. They believe God is capable of doing some of the most vicious, cruel, despicable things imaginable—criminal actions that would land them in jail or the electric chair if they were convicted of doing them according to the laws of our ungodly society today. Imagine a holy, loving, sinless God, guilty of crimes that most sinful, imperfect people would not consider doing to another human being, much less to one of their own children. Yet these people believe that God selfishly plucks babies and children out of their parent's arms because He needs a new flower in heaven; that He puts disease on His children to teach them a spiritual lesson; that He keeps His children in poverty to humble them, that He is the author of wars, murders, disease, accidents, earthquakes, hurricanes, floods and actions of the most evil nature.

A newspaper account of the funeral after the tragic death of an outstanding, eighteen-year-old, Christian athlete quoted one of the speakers at the memorial service as saying, "(the boys name) had so many talents, God probably needed them up there." [2]

No, God needs our talents down here on this earth to accomplish His Will and reach this world with the Gospel. How could the boy's earthly talents be used in Heaven anyhow? Although the words were meant to comfort the grieving family of the boy, they inadvertently made a statement about God that depicts Him as arbitrarily taking children away from their parents. Sinners look at that and wonder why anyone would want to serve that kind of a God. They want their children **protected** from that kind of behavior!

"Dear Abby: I have a 10-year-old daughter who is legally blind and mentally retarded. 'Maria' is able to walk and talk, but she has the mind of a 2 year old. She is almost as big as I am, and I have to feed, bathe, diaper and dress her. I can't leave her alone for a minute. I am 33 years old and have no life of my own.

"Maria is physically abusive. Baby sitters quit after one day...Abby, I love her. She is my child, but I can't understand why God did this to me. [3]

Although our heart aches for this dear mother, is it fair to blame her daughter's condition on God?

An Act Of God?

Concerning the Blizzard of 1996, "'This (storm) is the sort of thing they were thinking about when they wrote the 'Act of God' clause on the airbill.' says Federal Express spokesman William Carroll, referring to the provisions that allows the carrier to void its overnight guarantee." [4]

"Despite the Bible's assurance that 'rain falls on the just and on the unjust,' nearly 1 in 5 people believe recent floods are God's punishment." [5]

"Holi, (India) and nine other nearby villages were flattened Thursday by an earthquake in southwestern India that brought down flimsy homes, mangling and crushing victims in their sleep.

"But in this country of Hindu fatalism and belief in predetermination, (Ankush) Gaekwad isn't bitter, and he doesn't think that he should be angry with Ganesh the god of good luck.

"It was God's will. He gave us life. He will take it away, he said." [6]

It is interesting that people who believe God causes disasters are partially accepting some of the fatalistic doctrines of Hinduism in dealing with disasters?

After listening to and reading what some of the major Christian ministries have to say about disasters it would seem to be the case. One ministry writes, "Do you believe as I do that God is behind all the calamities and severe weather striking the United States? God is screaming at this nation and its leaders to repent—to stop the stampede toward humanism, atheism and godlessness!"

Of course God is against humanism, atheism and godlessness, but does He **initiate** these disasters, which kill hundreds of people, to get people's attention and cause them to repent? Not according to what Jesus had to say about His Father. It is true that after the fact, God's Holy Spirit does call people's attention to the fact that life is short and that people must get right with God if they want to have eternal life, but Jesus earmarked stealing, killing and destroying as the work of Satan. (John 10:10)

A False Prophecy

"Monday was the appointed day of doom, the day a street preacher said Portland would be devastated by an earthquake in retribution for unholy deeds.

"Street preacher John Gunter had said God told him the city would be destroyed May 3, (1993) by a quake. In March, Gunter sent a letter to churches in the region, saying Portland was ripe for judgment because it is a center for Satanic activity." [7]

In the letter to the pastors dated March 31, 1993 he stated, "(Portland) is a major if not **the** major center for Satanic activity in this nation...God has reserved this city for a day and an hour in order to set forth as an example to the rest of this nation what will happen if it does not repent!"

Not only did the quake not take place May 3, 1993, but the character of God was maligned once more and the Church was ridiculed by the very ones who need to be reached with the Gospel.

Carol and I spent nearly the entire day taking care of business in Portland on May 3rd that year because we know what God does and does not do. Numbers of Christians fled the city which points up the great need for teaching on this subject.

"In a poll reported by EP News Service, the Barna

researchers found that 86 percent of Americans believe God will judge people, and 74 percent believe this strongly.

"'The idea of Judgment Day is very firmly implanted within the church in America...The notion of God's grace is in a much more precarious position.

"Barna continued, 'It is also likely that this distortion is reducing the ability of the church to reach those outside it. Among unchurched adults a huge percentage—40 percent—believe God is not able to forgive all sins. These people are hearing messages of judgment from the church, but not messages of forgiveness. Is it such a surprise that they are staying away?'"[8]

An AIDS survey by the Kaiser Family Foundation found that, "...12% believe that AIDS came from God to punish homosexual behavior;"[9]

Did Jesus Teach That Disasters Are From God?

But disasters and this kind of teaching were not a part of Jesus' ministry when He was on this earth. Jesus brought the revolutionary news to earth that His Father is a loving God who wants to protect us from the handiwork of Satan.

"I once saw a cartoon that showed a scowling, bearded God pacing back and forth across a cloud with His hands clasped behind Him. Two timid angels were glancing at Him, and one was whispering to the other, 'He can't stand the idea of no-fault insurance.'

"The truth is, some people do picture God as the 'Celestial Grouch.' They seem to feel that He is constantly trying to throw thunderbolts at us, trying to zap us, trying to punish us for all of our wrongdoing.

"But that idea is devilish. Literally. That's what Satan wants us to think. His first lie in Eden was designed to plant a tiny seed of distrust in Eve's mind. 'Are you sure God is reliable?'

"It is simply not true that God is crotchety and mean. No one has ever accused Jesus of that, after all, and God and Jesus are one (see John 10:30)." [10]

Hebrews 1:3 says that Jesus is, "...the express image of his (Father's) person..." The word "image" means, the "...exact expression, or impression as when metal is pressed into a die, or as a seal upon wax." This indicates that if Jesus did not do evil things, His Father does not do them either. [11]

I really like what Pastor Jack Hayford told the press after the 1994 earthquake in Los Angeles. "One man who survived the Northridge quake called it a 'rumble from hell.' Some Christians in Los Angeles are calling it 'God's wake-up call.'

"Others view the disaster as God's judgment on the City of Angels for its sin...

"Others hold a more redemptive view of the earthquake...Jack Hayford, senior pastor of the Church on the Way in Van Nuys, says he believes recent problems could trigger a spiritual breakthrough for Los Angeles.

"Hayford is convinced that prayer kept the damage of the earthquake from being worse than it was.

"I don't believe it was God's hand that shook the earth, but I do believe His hand prevented the situation from being worse than it was." (author's emphasis) [12]

The Sons Of Thunder

James and John had their theology rearranged by Jesus

one day in Samaria. "And it came to pass, when the time was come that he should be received up, he steadfastly set his face to go to Jerusalem. And sent messengers before his face: and they went, and entered into a village of the Samaritans to make ready for him. And they did not receive him, because his face was as though he would go to Jerusalem. And when his disciples James and John saw this, they said, Lord, wilt thou that we command fire to come down from heaven, and consume them, even as Elias did?" (Or in so many words, Let's wipe them out. Let's do it Old Testament style!)

"But he turned, and rebuked them, and said, ye know not what manner of spirit ye are of. For the Son of man is not come to destroy men's lives but to save them." (Luke 9:51-56)

You don't know what you are saying, He tells them. That's devil talk. That is the way the devil works. I don't want to kill people because that is a work of the devil. God's way of working is to save people, to give them abundant life. "The thief cometh not, but for to steal, and to kill, and to destroy; I am come that they might have life, and that they might have it more abundantly." (John 10:10)

This same attitude can be observed when Peter tried to defend Jesus against the mob in the Garden of Gethsemane. "And, behold, one of them which were with Jesus stretched out his hand, and drew his sword, and struck a servant of the high priest's, and smote off his ear. Then said Jesus unto him, Put up again thy sword into his place: for all they that take the sword shall perish with the sword." (Matthew 26:51,52) Luke adds, "And he touched his ear, and healed him." (Luke 22:51)

I Hope He Gets His!

How many Christians repeat the same error the disciples made when they pray for God to strike dead a certain dictator or Arab leader or political personality because he has done something evil. Or they tell the world that God caused people like that to die suddenly or be killed when something of that nature actually happens to them. In fact, it seems that whenever there is any kind of horrendous occurrence of nature, some Christians feel it is their responsibility to tell everyone that this was an action of God, as if they are members of a terrorist group that needs to take credit for the latest disaster they initiated. That kind of destructive, malevolent behavior is not the kind of actions that draw sinners to God. Sinners, in reality, are trying to get away from that sort of thing because their lives are already full of destruction and pain.

God Is Not A Child Abuser

God does not abuse His creation and He is not a child abuser. Our message to sinners should express that wonderful message. "If you will believe and live according to God's Word He will **protect** you from these works of the devil. The devil would like to kill you, destroy your possessions, wipe out your job, hurt your children and make you live in fear and bondage, but God offers you freedom and protection if you will obey Him and have faith in His Word. And the reason He does this is because He truly loves you."

That was the simple message we preached night after night for twenty years as missionaries in open-air crusades in Latin America. We found that sinners already know their lives are a living hell. They don't want to be threatened by a God of vengeance, they want to find Someone who will love them.

After preaching that message every night for two and one-half years in Managua, Nicaragua, not one member of our churches, who was living a righteous life, was killed when the earthquake destroyed Managua in 1972! On the contrary, astonishing miracles took place that saved their lives. That which we had promised on the authority of God's Word had protected them from death in a supernatural way!

People in one of the new crusade churches were warned by the Holy Spirit thirty days in advance that an earthquake was coming. So they prayed and fasted and bound the devil in the Name of Jesus and that area of Managua suffered no damage, although the full impact of the earthquake was felt!

God Is The Life Giver

The simple fact is that God gives life in abundance and Satan is the one who tries to take life from us. When we accept Christ, stay out of sin and the works of the flesh and believe and act on God's Word, we have God's promise that He will **deliver** us out of the clutches of the devil!

One of the many things Jesus did when He came to this earth was straighten out mankind's wrong ideas, perceptions and traditions about His Father. "To understand the picture or snapshot of Old Testament truth about God the Father, it is necessary to see the video of Jesus walking out God-in-the-flesh while He was on the earth." [13]

2 Peter 3:9 reveals God's primary purpose in dealing

with the human race. "The Lord is not slack concerning his promises, as some men count slackness; but is longsuffering to us-ward, not willing that any should perish, but that all should come to repentance." Would it not be foolish for God to kill the very ones He wants to save? If that had been the case in the past, how many Christians would never have lived long enough to get saved because of the sinful, despicable lives they lived before accepting Christ?

In the age of Grace we are living in today, "...whosoever shall call upon the name of the Lord shall be saved." (Romans 10:13) That clearly reveals the attitude of God's heart in dealing with people today.

God's Judgment Comes After Death

God **will** judge mankind for their sins, but He will do so **after death**. "And it is appointed unto men once to die, but after this the judgment." (Hebrews 9:27)

While people are still alive they receive the **wages** for their sin which is death. (Romans 6:23) The seed of death is contained in every sin. When sin is ingested into the individual by an act of their will, the seed of death sprouts and begins to grow. If the sin is not repented of and washed away by the Blood of Jesus, it will eventually kill the individual both physically and spiritually. **Many confuse this process of receiving death for sinning with God's judgment for sin, which is yet to come after death.**

Sinners receive their wages for sin now. They are being paid for what they have earned. But the time is coming when they will still have to face God's judgment after death. "The Lord knoweth how to deliver the godly out of temptation, and to reserve the unjust unto the day of judgment to be punished." (2 Peter 2:9)

"But," people say, "the Old Testament says God killed people or at least instructed others to do so. How can we believe anything else when the Bible says He did it?"

But the **entire** Bible does not support that characterization of God the Father. On the contrary, Jesus describes God as a loving Father welcoming back His prodigal son who had wasted his life and inheritance in riotous living. (Luke 15:13) Jesus came from the very presence of God with the astounding news that, "God is love." (1 John 4:8) The Pharisees had wandered so far from the truth that they never did accept this testimony. Unfortunately some Christians today are repeating the same error as the Pharisees because they have not taken into consideration what the entire Bible says about the subject.

Give Special Attention To What Jesus Said

Understand that the testimony of Jesus is first-hand, not second or third-hand. In a court of law, first-hand testimony is the only information acceptable for consideration by the court. Anything else is "hear-say" evidence and is not admissible as evidence. Without taking anything away from the Old Testament, the first-hand testimony of Jesus must take absolute precedent over that of the Old Testament.

Although the Old Testament's types and shadows are wonderful and appreciated by all, it is easy to make a mistake when dealing with shadows. Shadows are difficult to pin down because they do not contain solid definition. Therefore, we have to carefully use the light of the New Testament, as revealed by the revelation of Jesus Christ, to substantiate the shadows of the Old Testament and arrive at the truth they are seeking to reveal.

One of those "lights" is found in John 5:18-21. "Therefore the Jews sought the more to kill him, because he not only had broken the Sabbath, but said also that God was his Father, making himself equal with God. Then answered Jesus and said unto him, Verily, verily, I say unto you, The Son can do nothing of himself, but what he seeth the Father do: for what things soever he doeth, these also doeth the Son likewise." (vs. 18,19) Jesus states here that He could only do what He saw His Father do. Since Jesus did nothing that was evil, then it follows that His Father did no evil for Jesus to see and consequently do.

"For the Father loveth the Son, and shewth him all things that himself doeth: and he will shew him greater works than these, that ye may marvel." (v. 20) This is even more forceful. Because He loves His Son, Jesus, the Father opens Himself completely by showing Jesus everything He does. Nothing is hidden, which reinforces the previous verse that Jesus saw no evil in His Father in which to copy in His own earthly life and ministry.

These Signs Follow Those Who Believe

"For as the Father raiseth up the dead, and quickeneth them; even so the Son quickeneth whom he will." (v.21) What were the "greater works" of the previous verse that the Father was going to show Jesus? They were the healing of the sick and the raising of the dead, which demonstrates that the Father's compelling emotion and motivating desire in the human race is to give Life, not death. He doesn't kill people, but is the One who actually reverses the death process the devil has placed in motion through sin and gives Life to those who will accept the healings and miracles by faith in His Word.

Can God be a killer in the Old Testament and a loving Father in the New Testament? No. He must be one or the other because He does not change. If He is a loving Father in the New Testament, that is what He must be in the Old Testament. How do we reconcile this apparent conflict? By correctly interpreting the Word of Truth. Apparently there are areas in the Bible that need to be interpreted or Paul would not have found it necessary to caution the reader about dividing it correctly. When it is done as Paul instructs, there is no conflict between the Old and New Testaments. If there is conflict, a mistake has been made in the interpretation.

CHAPTER THREE

The two major laws of interpretation to rightly divide truth are: (1) context, and (2) weight of scripture.

An exceedingly simple example of this exercise in arriving at truth can be found in Matthew 27:5. The Bible says, speaking of Judas, "And he cast down the pieces of silver in the temple, and departed, and went and hanged himself." In another passage the Bible also states, "...Go, and do thou likewise." (Luke 10:37) Does that mean that someone can commit suicide, or self-murder, with the Bible's blessing? Absolutely not!

(1) By using the law of context and comparing the two scriptures above it can be easily seen that they have nothing in common with each other. The first describes what happened when Judas realized the terrible decision he had made in betraying Jesus. The second has to do with the parable of the Good Samaritan.

Therefore, although the Bible actually does say, "Judas...went and hanged himself," and "...Go, and do thou likewise," the two scriptures have different contexts and cannot be hooked together to make a point, or the doctrine that God condones suicide.

(2) Then the rest of the Bible is used to double check this conclusion. Where does the weight of scripture fall in the matter of suicide or self-murder? Here are what some of the scriptures have to say about it.

"...thou shalt do no murder..." (Matt. 19:18)

"...murderers...shall have their part in the lake which burneth with fire and brimstone: which is the second death." (Rev. 21:8)

"...no murderer hath eternal life abiding in him." (1 John 3:15)

What Is The Evidence Of The Bible?

The evidence is abundant in the Bible that the weight of scripture settles on the fact that God does not support suicide or self-murder. Thus the two laws of interpretation expose the error that would result if someone attempted to use the above two scriptures to justify that suicide is not a sin.

For those who have gone through the traumatic experience of having a family member or friend commit suicide, this information is not intended to add to your grief by telling you the individual is lost eternally. Only God knows that. We have heard the testimonies of those who tried to commit suicide and lived to tell about it. Some of them told of using means, such as drugs or jumping off high places to try to take their life, which left them time to think about what they were doing before the effect or impact took place. When they realized the finality of their action, some cried out to God to forgive them of their sin as they were falling through the air or before they passed out.

We believe God forgives murderers in prison for their sin when they repent so why wouldn't He also forgive self-murderers who repent if they have sufficient time? The point is that we cannot judge other people. Only God knows the thoughts of man, but the principle still holds true that the Bible cannot be used to justify suicide.

We Are New Testament Believers

Then it must be understood that believers in Jesus Christ today are New Testament Christians. The Old Testament contains an old covenant that has been fulfilled. "Think not that I am come to destroy the law, or the prophets: I am not come to destroy, but to fulfill." (Matt. 5:17) The Greek word for "fulfill" is "plero" which means, "to satisfy, expire, and to end by fulfilling like other prophecies when fulfilled." [1]

Hebrews says, "In that he saith, a new covenant, he hath made the first old. Now that which decayeth and waxeth old is ready to vanish away." (8:13) The Greek word for "old" is "palaioo" which means, "to abrogate; annul; be antiquated; no longer in force; to be obsolete, out of date." [2]

That does not signify that the Old Testament is not the inspired Word of God. And, of course it must be understood that God's Laws are still in force today. But it does demonstrate where the emphasis must be placed in today's time frame. Jesus has provided a New Covenant by His death and resurrection which has fulfilled the ceremonial and sacrificial demands of the Law, thereby making it possible to go directly to Him to receive forgiveness for our sins now instead of offering an animal blood sacrifice.

There are those Christians who find it difficult to understand that their doctrines and beliefs are not to be centered on Old Testament scripture, but on the New Testament. They must carefully ascertain that what they think the Old Testament says is fully supported by what the New Testament teaches before they form any kind of doctrine. The Old Testament must be rightly divided in the light of New Testament truth. Why focus on the shadow or type of what is to come, when that which the shadow was pointing to for centuries is here? Now the laws of God are written on our hearts, not on tablets of stone. (2 Cor. 3:3) Jesus brought a new revelation down from Heaven that is more finely-tuned than the Old Testament revelation. To illustrate this in the natural realm, a patient would certainly not permit a surgeon to perform brain surgery using knowledge of the 1800's when present-day, modern technology and methods are available.

Interpreting The Old Testament

"All Scripture is inspired, but some parts are subject to illumination by other parts. For example: the New Testament interprets the Old Testament. To place the Old Testament over the New is cultic. Religion is not summed up in the Ten Commandments. Worship is on the first day of the week, not the seventh. Christ supersedes the burnt offerings. We understand the Old Testament through the New." [3]

"Interpretation of the Old Testament does not dispute

what was 'said,' but rather what was 'meant'. This is impossible without the New Testament revelation that sheds light on the character of God and the economy in which people lived. The limitation of revelation knowledge will result in incomplete conclusions." [4]

The book of Galatians was written to New Testament believers who had fallen back into the Old Testament rite of circumcision after having placed their faith in Jesus for their salvation. Paul called them "foolish" for having done so. (Gal. 3:1) Entire church denominations have made the same mistake today when they embrace the Jewish Sabbath and the Old Testament dietary laws, for example, as the bases for their beliefs instead of New Testament truth.

So, in judging the character of God one cannot fall into the habit of looking exclusively to the Old Testament for information. Compared to the Father which Jesus revealed in the New Testament, the Old Testament information appears quite different when not interpreted correctly.

For instance, the Hebrews of the Old Testament believed that God did both good and evil. That is one reason the Old Testament has so many references to God doing things in the Old Testament which are incompatible with the teachings Jesus gave in the New Testament about His Father.

Who Did What?

The case of David numbering Israel is one such illustration. 2 Samuel 24:1 says, "And again the anger of the Lord was kindled against Israel and He moved David against them to say, Go number Israel and Judah." Here God is blamed for causing David to sin by placing his confidence in numbers instead of in God.

But look at 1 Chronicles 21:1, which speaks about the same incident and gives a distinctly different version of who caused David to sin. "And Satan stood up against Israel and provoked David to number Israel."

This points up the difficulty of ascertaining in the Old Testament just what God did and did not do. Because the revelation about God was clouded, He was blamed on many occasions for actions in the Old Testament which were actually the work of the devil, as seen above in 2 Sam. 24:1.

Then how do we know what is the correct view? By rightly dividing the Word of Truth.

What does the New Testament say about God causing people to sin? James 1:13 says, "Let no one say when he is tempted, I am tempted from God; for God is incapable of being tempted by [what is] evil and He Himself tempts no one." (Amplified Bible) So the truth is that God did not motivate David to number Israel causing him to sin, Satan did!

The New Testament is very clear about who does the tempting. When Jesus was led into the wilderness by the Spirit He was tempted by the devil. (Matt. 26:41) Not only is Satan the tempter, but God is revealed as the One who delivers people from temptation in the Lord's Prayer. "Do not permit us to be overcome by evil but deliver us from the evil one." [5]

What About Job?

Another example of the belief in the Old Testament that God did both good and evil is the case of Job. He said, "...the Lord gave, and the Lord hath taken away; blessed be the name of the Lord." (Job 1:21) Or, God gave me my children, wealth and health and then took them all back. But is that statement correct? Did God take anything away from Job? Did God kill Job's children and animals and put boils on his body? No, Satan did. (Job 1:12)

Job's estimation of what was happening at that time was incorrect. The Bible tells things the way they happened, whether they were right or wrong, and it is up to the reader to know the Bible well enough to rightly divide the truth from the error in such cases. The fact is that Job made 74 charges against God which were false. (Appendix 1, p. 171)

Here are two of the 74 incorrect charges Job made against God. (1) Job said, "Thou scarest me with dreams and terrifiest me through visions." (Job 7:14) The truth is that God does not give people nightmares and cause them to be fearful. That is the work of Satan. "For God hath not given us the spirit of fear but of power, and of love and of a sound mind." (2 Tim. 1:7) (2) In Job 7:21 Job said, "Why dost thou not pardon my transgression, and take away mine iniquity?" Once again Job was mistaken because God does forgive our sins. "If we confess our sins, he is faithful and just to forgive us our sins, and to cleanse us from all unrighteousness." (1 John 1:9) Job made his incorrect statement because he had believed the lie of Satan that God wouldn't forgiving his sins.

Unfortunately, some people go back to the book of Job and pick out these false accusations, attempting to use them to prove that God still employs such tactics in people's lives today if He so chooses. But it is dangerous to take the words of a man who was under extreme pressure, going through a meat-grinder experience, without the support of a Bible, a church, a pastor or any of the knowledge of God which is contained in the New Testament, and use what he mistakenly said under those circumstances to form doctrines and beliefs today. Certainly no one would want people to take what they say today, when they are having a bad day, under pressure and out of sorts, and make that a standard by which all Christians should conduct themselves. For that reason the Book of Job must be carefully interpreted in the light of the New Testament to arrive at what is the actual truth.

Some would say, "But God allowed Job to be tested. Maybe He didn't directly cause Job's problems, but he permitted them to happen to see if Job really loved Him."

Does God Do This?

But is that the way God rewards goodness? God said of Job, "...there is none like him in the earth, a perfect and upright man, one that feareth God, and escheweth evil." (Job 1:8) The Hebrew word for "perfect" could be better understood as, "undefiled." (Strong's, word 8535) Job was not perfect in the sense of sinless perfection, but he was a good moral man who reverenced and obeyed God's Laws. He was such a righteous man that God was proud of him.

Does the weight of scripture in the Bible support the fact that God rewards good people like Job with evil? None whatsoever. God **protects** people from the devil who obey His Word and walk in His statutes. "We know [absolutely] that anyone born of God does not [deliberately and knowingly] practice committing sin, but the One Who was begotten of God carefully watches over and protects him [Christ's divine presence within him preserves him against the evil], and the wicked one does not lay hold (get a grip) on him or touch [him]." (I John 5:18, Amplified Bible)

Job's major spiritual problem was a **great** fear, which lowered the "hedge" around him and allowed the devil to do things to Job he could not have done if the hedge had been in place. "For the thing which I **greatly** feared is come upon me, and that which I was afraid of is come unto me." (Job 3:25) (Author's emphasis) Fear is a work of the devil and any work of the devil that is allowed to operate in our lives opens us up to the harassment of the devil. (2 Tim. 1:7)

This was not just any fear, it was a **GREAT** fear. He had fearfully anticipated the loss of his children, wealth and health. Satan was able to use the open door of fear to bring Job's negative vision of fear to pass just as God is able to bring a positive vision of faith to pass. Whoever we **will** to operate in our life, whether negative or positive, is the one who will dominate our life and family.

When Job eventually stopped trying to tell God what was wrong, forgave his friends and began listening, God was able to free Job from the captivity to fear that had precipitated the situation. (Job 40:4,5; 42:6,10)

But Some Good Things Happened

"But," people will say, "I have received so much good

as a result of being sick or recovering from an accident. I had more time to pray and read the Bible and I had marvelous visitations from the Lord. God must have at least permitted the sickness or accident so that I could learn what I did at that time."

No, God could have accomplished the same thing in their life if they would have taken the time to pray and read the Bible before the sickness or accident occurred. The fact that they were sick or injured was not the reason they learned the lesson, but the fact that they now had the time to **listen** to what God had been trying to get through to them all along.

To say that God can relate to His children in a better way when they are sick and hurt would be the same as if parents beat their children with a baseball bat so they would listen to them more attentively and learn more because of the beating. That kind of abuse would not only land the parents in jail for child abuse, but would create hatred and resentment in their children's hearts. **And that is one of the reasons God does not abuse His children either!**

Let's face it, God is a master Teacher. He knows how to teach us a lesson that will get the point through to us in the best possible way without lowering Himself to the level of Satan's abusive tactics.

God's method or means of educating His children is to teach them out of His Word, by His Holy Spirit. "Thy word is a lamp unto my feet, and a light unto my pathway." (Psalms 119:105) "But the Comforter, which is the Holy Ghost, whom the Father will send in my name, he shall teach you all things, and bring all things to your remembrance, whatsoever I have said unto you." (John 14:26)

Most parents teach their children that they should not play in the street because a car could come along and seriously injure them. If the children would listen carefully to their parents they could learn the lessons very easily, without complications. But if they still persist in playing in the street, one day a car will hit them and they will learn what the parents had been trying to teach them all along.

I Have This Child Who Needs To Learn A Lesson

Parents would never choose or arrange for a car to hit their children to teach them a lesson because they love them, which was the motivating emotion for warning them of the danger in the first place. But when it does happen, the children realize their parents knew what they were talking about and will now listen carefully to their parent's instructions about not playing in the street.

As a result of the accident, the children have time to think about the consequences of their unwise action as they recover. Not only that, but they are more attentive now to listen to their parent's teaching about life in general. The sad fact is that the children could have learned all they needed to learn without being hit by the car if they would have just listened to and obeyed their parent's instructions.

The fact that God permits or allows something to happen does not mean He **arranges** for them to happen. There is a world of difference between the two. If a man wants to rob a bank, God will permit him to do so. He will not approve of it, but God will not stand in the bank doorway and physically stop him. Why? Because He has given the man a free will to choose what he wills to do. He will permit him to rob the bank, but He certainly will never arrange for him to do it just to teach him that robbing banks is wrong.

Of course the bank robber will eventually be captured and face the results of robbing the bank. He will pay for his crime by being locked in jail for the appropriate length of time. While in jail he will have plenty of time to repent of his sins, read the Bible and pray.

In fact, some people get saved in prison. But God didn't arrange for them to break the Law so they would have the opportunity to get saved. That would mean that God was involved in causing the people to sin. He prefers that they get saved while they are free. But after the crime is committed, the sentence is pronounced and the criminal is placed behind bars, if He is invited, God will enter the scene and cause good to come out of a bad situation by saving the criminal from his sins.

It may be true that the criminal might have never gotten saved if he had not been thrown into prison, but that is not within God's area of responsibility. God has made Salvation available for anyone who is willing to receive it at any time. After that, it is up to the individual to accept or reject Salvation whenever and wherever he may choose and God honors that choice, whichever way it may be.

God Told Me To Do It

Just because God permits or allows something to happen in a person's life does not signify that those evil things which happen as a result of his bad choices are God's will for his life. I've heard people spiritualize their mistakes and problems by saying God told them to do it, thereby shifting the blame onto God for their bad judgment or sin. "God permitted me to go through that sickness, or business failure, or automobile accident or fill-in-the-blank circumstance so that this or that could take place in my life."

In reality, it is a rerun of Adam's old excuse for why he ate the fruit of the tree of the knowledge of good and evil, "And the man (Adam) said, The woman whom thou gavest to be with me, she gave me of the tree, and I did eat." (Genesis 3:12) And people have been "passing the buck" ever since. The unfortunate fallout from this spiritual irresponsibility is that it casts a shadow of evilness on God for, "...allowing such terrible things to happen to His children."

Permissive Vs. Causative Tenses

A further consideration of whether God permitted or caused evil things to happen in the Old Testament must include the fact that there are areas of the Hebrew and English languages that are not compatible, as the case is in most language comparisons. "Dr. Robert Young, author of *Young's Analytical Concordance to the Bible*, sheds some crucial light on that and other similar scriptures in his book, *Hints to Bible Interpretation.* There he explains that the Hebrew language contains idioms which cannot be translated into the English language and properly understood. Also, there was little understanding of permissive and causative verbs."[6]

For instance, Deuteronomy 28:15 correctly states that curses will come upon people who disobey God's commands and statutes. Romans 6:23 calls that the wages of sin, "For the wages of sin is death; but the gift of God is eternal life through Jesus Christ our Lord."

But then, beginning with verse 20 it says, "The Lord shall send upon thee cursing, vexation, and rebuke, in all that thou settest thine hand unto for to do, until thou be destroyed, and until thou perish quickly;" Verse 61 continues in the same tone, "Also every sickness, and every plague, which is not written in the book of this law, them will the Lord bring upon thee, until thou be destroyed."

But God Isn't The Author Of Sickness And Disease

It would appear from these verses that God is the author of sickness and disease as well as many other evil things. But that is not true according to the revelation of the New Testament. Jesus informs us that it is the devil who kills and destroys, not God. (John 10:10) The only thing Jesus ever cursed on this earth was a fig tree. He spent His entire ministry **blessing** people, not cursing them.

God isn't the curse of the Law, **sin is**, and diseases came into existence as a result of sin. In reality, it isn't necessary for God to put anything on people because the curse will come on them automatically. The curse is more than willing to do it all by itself.

The answer to the apparent dilemma is simply that in the original text it is better to say that God would not "permit" the disease to come upon them. The truth is that God protects people from disease who obey His Word. But if they do not obey His Word, He cannot provide the protection over them He would like to give because they have placed themselves in a compromising position by disobeying or failing to believe God's commands and statutes or are ignorant of their rights as a child of God.

"' But even if God is not the source of sickness,' someone may ask, 'Isn't it still true that He allows the devil to make us sick?'

"Yes. Not from the standpoint of correction, but from the standpoint of authority. God allows it because we do. Why? Because He's given us the right to make our own choices along with authority over the kingdom of darkness in Jesus' Name.

"Notice what God said in Deuteronomy 30:19: 'I call heaven and earth to record this day against you, that I have set before you life and death, blessing and cursing: therefore choose life, that both thou and thy seed may live.' The choice of whether we experience life or death, blessings or curses is up to us. It has been this way since creation.

"When God created Adam, He gave him the ability and the privilege of making his own decisions. Adam never experienced sickness until, of his own free will, he disobeyed God. As a result of his disobedience, he came under the rule of a new 'god' and a new kingdom—Satan and the kingdom of darkness. Sickness was a byproduct of this new kingdom. Sickness was not a tool in the hand of God to teach Adam a lesson. It was the harvest of the seed of disobedience, part of the kingdom of darkness." [7]

Jesus Delivered Us From The Curse Of The Law

That action on the part of Adam and Eve caused the entire human race to be plunged into sin, which brought about the need for the redemption of mankind from the power of Satan. Redemption required Jesus to go to the cross where He took our place, paid the price for our sin, and took the stripes on His back for the healing of our sicknesses and diseases.

To even intimate that God would have anything to do with sickness and disease being put back on the human race, something which cost His Son so much to purchase, is to insult the integrity of God no matter what the reason might be for doing so!

A further sampling of other passages that seem to contradict what Jesus said about His Father are: (1) "I form the light, and create darkness: I make peace, and create evil: I the Lord do all these things." (Isaiah 45:7) (2) "Shall a trumpet be blown in the city, and the people not be afraid? Shall there be evil in the city, and the Lord hath not done it?" (Amos 3:6) Once again the permissive sense should have been used instead of the causative. The truth of the New Testament is that God does not do anything which is evil, much less create evil. How could a Holy, Loving, Sinless God bring evil into existence?

Ezekiel placed the blame where it belongs. He said that iniquity or sin was first found in the heart of the anointed cherub. "Thou wast perfect in thy ways from the day that thou wast created, till iniquity was found in thee." (Ezekiel 28:15) Lucifer, of his own free will, invented sin and as a result became the evil, fallen creature, Satan. **That is where evil originated!**

(3) "Then there came out a spirit, and stood before the Lord, and said, I will entice him. And the Lord said unto him, Wherewith? And he said I will go out, and be a lying spirit in the mouth of all his prophets. And the Lord said, Thou shalt entice him, and thou shalt also prevail: go out, and do even so. Now therefore, behold, the Lord hath put a lying spirit in the mouth of these thy prophets, and the Lord

hath spoken evil against thee." (2 Chron. 18:20-22)

What Is Wrong With This Picture?

Something is obviously wrong here because this passage goes against everything Jesus said about His Father. God cannot be Truth and be involved in a "good old boy" type of situation like this. Truth cannot contradict itself or it ceases to be Truth. God will not put a lying spirit in anyone's mouth because that would be insinuating that God forced them to lie, which is a sin, and God does not force anyone to sin.

"Let no man say when he is tempted, I am tempted of God: for God cannot be tempted with evil, neither tempteth he any man: But every man is tempted, when he is drawn away of his own lust, and enticed. Then when lust hath conceived, it bringeth forth sin: and sin, when it is finished, bringeth forth death." (James 1:13-15) If God cannot be tempted with evil it would be absurd to think He created evil. The whole idea of God having anything to do with evil and sin is diametrically opposed to the Character of God.

A look at the context is all that is needed to interpret what was really going on in this passage. Ahab, king of Israel, did not want to hear from God or His true prophets in any way whatsoever. So he gathered "prophets" around him who told him what he wanted to hear. To those who did not understand the true situation, it appeared as though "God's" prophets were lying as they prophesied in Ahab's court. But God's prophets do not lie. God would not command His prophets to speak only the truth and then force them to lie.

Satan Is The Father Of Lies

If any lies are involved, you can be absolutely certain God is not involved in it. Jesus gives the source of all lies when He informed the Pharisees, "Ye are of your father, the devil, and it is your will to practice the lusts and gratify the desires [which are characteristic] of your father. He was a murderer from the beginning and does not stand in the truth, because there is no truth in him. When he speaks a falsehood, he speaks what is natural to him, for he is a liar [himself] and the father of lies and of all that is false." (John 8:44, Amplified Bible)

(4) "The Lord hath mingled a perverse spirit in the midst thereof: and they have caused Egypt to err in every work thereof, as a drunken man staggereth in his vomit." (Isaiah 19:14) This scripture accuses God of directing a perverse spirit to make Egypt sin. But the evidence of God's Word proves that He does not need the help of perverse spirits to accomplish His Will on this earth. He has the Holy Spirit, who is perfectly capable of doing everything that needs to be done. A clearer understanding of this passage would be that because of Egypt's continual sin, God took His Hands off the situation, allowing the perverse spirit to lead the nation into all kinds of problems.

"The straw that broke the proverbial camel's back is found in the third verse (of Isaiah 19) where it says the Egyptians sought the help of idols, charmers, familiar spirits and wizards. That is an automatic hands-off signal wherever God is concerned. He will not tolerate a divided allegiance.

"The first chapter of Romans is the New Testament equivalent of the above mentioned Egyptian debacle. 'And even as they did not like to retain God in their knowledge, God gave them over to a reprobate mind, to do those things which are not convenient;' (Romans 1:28)."[8]

God Is So Good

The psalmist caught a true glimpse of God the Father 'hen he said, "The Lord is gracious and full of compas-)n; slow to anger, and of great mercy. The Lord is good to and his tender mercies are over all his works." (Psalms :8,9)

"(For the Lord thy God is a merciful God;) he will sake thee, neither destroy thee, nor forget the cov- thy fathers which he sware unto them." (Deut. 4:31)

) have a true understanding of who God is and to v Him, God must be judged by His Characteristics es, which do not change from the Old to the New God says of Himself, "For I am the Lord, I change chi 3:6) In His Word, God clearly portrays His Characteristics or Attributes that He wants to nkind to this point. This is not putting God in a aying that this is all God will ever be.

Revelation Has Been Gradual

the darkness of man's mind and his dis- positi God chose to unfold Himself in lim- ited me ntil the revelation became a part of people's live nfold more about Himself.

"Through Noah, God restored the knowledge that He enjoys communication with people. Abraham entered into that communication and learned that God is also a God of covenants. Years later, Moses, having participated in these two revelations of God, discovered that God is a moral God concerned with man's good, and Joshua experienced the almightiness of God. This formed a basis for further revelation, so that Isaiah met a holy God, Ezekiel met a glorious God and Daniel met a revealing God.

"We need not wait until 'the sweet by and by' to know the God who was so real and personal to Adam; ever since Adam walked in the garden, God has been giving back that wonderful knowledge of Himself, until we now have the second Adam, Jesus Christ, in us the hope of glory. God may not walk with us in the flesh, but He is even closer to us as He indwells our spirits." [9]

One of the wonderful privileges of heaven will be that God will continue revealing Himself to His children throughout the endless ages of eternity!

CHAPTER FOUR

Abraham is an example of a man who knew God. Because he understood God's character he did not become traumatized or disoriented in his faith when God told him to sacrifice his only son, Isaac, as a burnt offering.

Isaac was a gift from God; a miracle child born when Abraham was 100-years-old and his wife, Sarah, was 90. God had promised Abraham that through Isaac his descendants would be as numerous as the sands of the sea and the stars in the heaven. So it was extremely important that Isaac live if God's promise was to be realized.

Abraham was sure that God **always** keeps His promises so he had the absolute assurance in his heart that Isaac would somehow live through this experience despite the fact that God had commanded him to kill his only son of promise. (Heb. 11:17-19) We know that Abraham was aware of this fact by the answer He gave when Isaac pointed out to him that they had everything they needed for the burnt offering except the lamb. He responded, "...My son, God will provide himself a lamb for the burnt offering:" (Genesis 22:8)

The strength of Abraham's faith was awesome to behold as he reached for the knife, picked it up and drew it back in the classic killing position. But Isaac's faith was also notable as he lay silent, helpless on the altar, under the shadow of the knife blade. At that moment, God quickly stopped Abraham. We know that Abraham had anticipated that something of this nature would occur because he had already instructed the servant who had accompanied them, "Abide ye here with the ass; and I and the lad will go yonder and worship, and come again to you." (Gen. 22:5) There was no doubt in Abraham's mind that he and Isaac would come back to where the servant was waiting for them.

That is exactly what happened. God provided a ram for the sacrifice and renewed His promise with Abraham that his descendents would be as numberless as the sands of the sea.

The Covenant Relationship

Why would God make such a demand to begin with? The answer to that question can be found by examining the covenant relationship between Abraham and God.

"A covenant had to be 'proved' or a seal had to be put upon it. This was done through an exchange of the oldest child of each partner. 'After these events, God tested and proved Abraham, and said to him, Abraham! And he said, Here I am' (Gen. 22:1 AMP). God had to test or prove the covenant with Abraham. The test was to see if Abraham, as a covenant partner, would stand firm." [1]

The motivating factor in presenting this scenario to Abraham was that God planned for His only begotten Son to die for the sins of the world. For the covenant to be kept, Abraham had to also be willing to sacrifice his only son.

However, the sacrifice of God's Son was in another dimension and quantum lengths beyond anything the sacrifice of Isaac could have ever hoped to accomplish. Isaac was certainly not the perfect, spotless sacrifice that Jesus would be, which would satisfy the Justice of God for the payment of sin that the Law demanded. Therefore this could not be the normal exchange of one son for the other.

God would also never dabble in the human sacrificial rites of the heathen and those involved in witchcraft and satanism. Judgment always fell on those nations who practiced such things. Would God ask Abraham to do something which He judged other nations for doing? No, God's purpose in all of this was not the death of Isaac, but that Abraham should obey without question the rules of the covenant.

Isaac Was Special

Isaac was the son of promise. There could be no other. God would have broken His Word if Isaac had been killed on His orders. So, when the situation progressed to the point that Abraham's actions proved conclusively that he was willing to keep the covenant, the Mercy of God swung into action.

"Abraham, since you have already sacrificed Isaac in your heart, you've demonstrated your complete willingness to sacrifice your child. Because you have been willing to sacrifice your only son, you've validated the covenant; now I can sacrifice My only Son." [2]

Abraham had no idea of the far-reaching effects his faith and obedience to God would have on this occasion, other than the fact that he had kept his side of the covenant. When Abraham met the demands of the covenant that were humanly possible, God was obligated to accomplish His side of the agreement, which resulted in the redemption of the human race through His Son, Jesus. For that obedience and faith Abraham became not only the father of a nation, but the father of **our** faith.

Abraham's understanding of God, His character and His actions enabled him to go through a potentially traumatic experience and come out of it with a faith that was stronger than ever. That is why it is so important that we have more than a superficial understanding of and relationship with God.

I Never Really Knew My Father Until...

Rev. William (Bill) Gallaher, Superintendent of the Oregon District of the Assemblies of God, learned the value of truly knowing God through his earthly father. Bill grew up in a military family. His father was a Naval officer stationed in Hawaii when the Japanese bombed Pearl Harbor. He tells the rest of the story in his own words.

"My dad was home that morning and we heard the guns going off and the bombs dropping. He left home and we didn't see him again for three years, and then we saw him for only snatches of time. I recognized him when he came into the house, but because he hadn't been home I didn't really know him. I resented him because my best friend's dad apparently had chosen to be home with his family, but my dad had chosen not to be home with us. Consequently, I made up some ideas about my dad without even knowing him.

"When I was twelve-years-old my dad retired and took over the house. But he didn't know how to be a dad because he hadn't been around children. I thought, 'Who is this guy to come in and order me around.' I knew what my dad looked like, I ate at his table, he took me to school and bought my clothes, and I could say he was my father, but I didn't really know him.

"It wasn't until after I had accepted the Lord as my Savior and was about 30 years old that God began to deal with me about our relationship. I began to hunger to really know my dad, my earthly father. I complained to God about it and God told me, 'That's not your father's problem, its your problem because you are the Christian.' So I began to pursue a better relationship which eventually led to my dad's salvation. My wife led him to the Lord before he passed away.

"I didn't really know, though, what my father's real thoughts were until my mother passed away. In settling the estate I opened a big cedar chest and there, to my surprise, were piles of letters from my dad, all neatly wrapped with red ribbons. The letters were in World War II airmail style envelopes, written in ink and packaged by the month.

"When I began reading them it was like opening a whole, new book for me. I found out things I didn't know about my dad and as I sat there, tears began to course down my cheeks. For the first time in my life I discovered through the letters that my dad had really loved me. I'm not blaming him, I'm blaming myself. I found for the first time that he really had been concerned about the fact that he wasn't with us during the war; that it hadn't been his choice to be absent; that he had wished that he could have been with his family. But it had taken me many years to find it out!" [3]

How many Christians have the same problem with their Heavenly Father? They know about Him and even some of the things He does in their lives, but they have many strange ideas about Him and even resentments toward Him because they don't really know Him. They haven't pursued Him by reading His Letter that reveals the love He has in His heart for His children. Therefore, their relationship with their Heavenly Father is not a healthy one and they are open to satanic deception because of their doubts, suspicions and fears. They believe the devil's lies that their Heavenly Father is cruel, abusive, unloving, vindictive, mean-spirited and evil, when He is really the best Friend they will ever have.

Other Christians only see a certain side of God. They do not see the full spectrum of the Rainbow, only certain colors. Their religious denominational blind-spots and prejudices filter out some of the "colors" of God that could enrich their lives beyond imagination. So they are robbed of the full scope of the relationship God desires to have with them.

People who know God, His Character, His Attributes, and what He has promised in His Word will be able to stand in the midst of the storm and know that God will do exactly what He has promised He will do in His Word if His conditions are met. There will be no blaming of God for those things Satan has actually done to them nor will they attribute to Satan those things God has done for them. They will have a deep, abiding confidence in God that He, "...will never leave thee, nor forsake thee." (Hebrews 13:5) "...and there is a friend that sticketh closer than a brother." (Proverbs 18:24)

An Important Rule Of Interpretation

The truth about God therefore cannot be ascertained by taking a scripture and saying that because the scripture says a certain thing, that is reason enough to believe it is an action of God. The correct manner to rightly divide or interpret the Word is to begin **first** with God's Character and **then work back from that point**. Does the **scripture** agree with God's Character? If it doesn't, then what is the reason why it does not agree? What is the context? Where does the weight of scripture rest? What did Jesus say about such things regarding His Father? **The scripture must agree with God's Character because God does not change from one scripture to the next**!

So let's begin examining the Character or Attributes of God to find out who God is, and as a result, what God does and does not do. "Character may be defined as a consistent pattern of behavior and attitudes."[4]

We know each other by our character. If we have a friend who has a character defect, such as not paying his bills, we would be foolish to loan him any money, unless we just wanted to give it away, because his character dictates what his actions will be. If our friend likes to gossip we only tell him those things we wouldn't mind sharing with the whole world. On the other hand, if our friend has proven his ability to keep a secret, we are able to trust him with valuable information. So it is with God. Can we trust Him totally or will He let us down when we can least afford it? I believe when we see and understand the entire spectrum of God's Character we will never doubt Him again and our relationship with Him will be revolutionized!

The Attributes Of God

In understanding God, one of the many qualities to consider is that He is a **SPIRIT**. That is His very essence. "God is a spirit: and they that worship him must worship him in spirit and in truth." (John 4:24) He has no body as humans do and therefore is invisible to the human eye. "Behold my hands and my feet, that it is I myself: handle me, and see; for a spirit hath not flesh and bones, as ye see me have." (Luke 24:39)

But He does have some kind of spiritual form just as people have when their spirit leaves their body after death and before they are united with their incorruptible body after the Rapture of the Church of Jesus Christ. "And the Father himself, which hath sent me, hath borne witness of me. Ye have neither heard his voice at any time, nor seen his shape." (John 5:37)

Then Paul tells us by the revelation of the Holy Spirit that Jesus had the same form God has before He came to earth to put on a human body. "Who, being in the form of God, thought it not robbery to be equal with God: But made himself of no reputation, and took upon him the form of a servant, and was made in the likeness of men:" (Phil. 2:6) Notice in this scripture that the "form" or "shape" which God has and the "likeness of men" that Jesus had to take upon Himself are different to the point that it was necessary to distinguish between the two forms. Apparently it was a huge step for Jesus to take. (Spirits may not have a physical body but they do have the ability to assume a physical form when it is necessary to make physical contact with human beings.)

Although the Bible speaks of God as having body parts, those scriptures should probably be understood in the figurative sense to a certain degree. This approach served as a way of communicating with the human race on their level of understanding.

"...thus his face denotes his sight and presence,...His eyes signify his omniscience, and all-seeing providence;...His ears, his readiness to attend unto and answer the requests of his people, and deliver them out of their troubles,...His nose and nostrils, his acceptance of the persons and sacrifices of men,...or his disgust at them,...His mouth is expressive of his commands, promises, threatenings, and prophecies, delivered out by him,...His arms and hands signify his power, and the exertion of it, as in making the heavens and the earth,..." [5]

Spirits are also **ETERNAL**. God has neither beginning or end. He has always existed and always will exist. "...before me there was no God formed, neither shall there be after me." (Isa. 43:10) "I am the first, and I am the last; and beside me there is no God." (Isa. 44:6)

Because God is an eternal spirit, time and space do not affect him. "...be not ignorant of this one thing, that one day is with the Lord as a thousand years, and a thousand years as one day." (2 Peter 3:8)

God is independent of any other being. He is restrained only by His own character. Every other living being depends upon Him for their life and existence, but He depends upon no one for anything. If God should cease to exist, the entire Universe would also cease to exist.

The human mind cannot begin to understand this attribute of God. But for those who will accept Christ as their Savior and live according to His Word, He has promised them eternal life. They will live and reign with God throughout the endless ages of eternity.

God is **INFINITE**, which means that He is without limits because He is so immense, unfathomable and uncomprehendable. However, He does limit Himself in certain areas for our benefit as the case is, for example, with man's free will. If God did not do so, His Power is so great that every person in the world would instantly fall down and accept Christ as their Savior. But God desires that mankind accept Christ because they choose to do so and not because it is forced upon them. Therefore God deliberately restrains His Power so that people have the opportunity to decide for themselves.

God is **SOVEREIGN**, meaning that He is the absolute supreme ruler of the Universe.

"Infinitely elevated above the highest creature, He is the Most High, Lord of heaven and earth; subject to none, influenced by none, absolutely independent. God does as He pleases, only as He pleases, always as He pleases. None can thwart Him, none can hinder Him. So His own Word expressly declares: 'My counsel shall stand, and I will do all my pleasure' (Isaiah 6:10);" [6]

But in viewing all of His characteristics or attributes, we must also realize that although God is the absolute supreme ruler of the Universe, He does not behave in the manner of an earthly dictator. **He still acts within the framework of His Character**.

"There are some things which God cannot do because they are contrary to his nature as God. He cannot look with favor on iniquity (Hab. 1:13), deny himself (2 Tim. 2:13), lie (Titus 1:2, Heb. 6:18), or tempt or be tempted to sin (James 1:13). God has limited himself to some extent by giving free will to his rational creatures. That is why he did not keep sin out of the universe by a display of his power and why he does not save anyone by force." [7]

Yet, the unspoken thought of some theologians, theological professors, and even entire denominations is that because God is Sovereign, He has the right to do whatever He wishes, even to the point of doing evil deeds that can only be attributable to the devil when viewed in the light of Satan's character which will be discussed later. That can never be; God will never act in a satanic manner!

A Bad Hair Day

Humans may have bad days and do things that are "out-of-character" because they are under pressure, tired or just feel mean, but God **never, ever** does anything that is not within the framework of His character. He is the most balanced Personality in the Universe and mankind can have complete confidence in the fact that He will always remain so.

In addition to the above attributes or characteristics of God's inner nature, **SPIRIT, ETERNAL, INFINITE,** and **SOVEREIGN**, the following is a listing of God's active and moral attributes or characteristics as He has revealed Himself to this point in time in His Word.

GOD IS:

OMNISCIENT
OMNIPRESENT
OMNIPOTENT
IMMUTABLE/UNCHANGEABLE
HOLY/PURE
JUST/RIGHTEOUS
GOOD
- **a. LOVE**
- **b. LONG-SUFFERING/PATIENT**
- **c. MERCY**
- **d. GRACE**

TRUTH/FAITHFULNESS
LIFE
PROVIDENT
ANGER/WRATH

For a more in-depth look at the list, we'll begin with **OMNISCIENT**, the possession of all knowledge.

"O the depth of the riches both of the wisdom and knowledge of God! how unsearchable are his judgments, and his ways past finding out! For who hath known the mind of the Lord? or who hath been his counselor? Or who hath first given to him, and it shall be recompensed unto him again? For of him, and through him, and to him, are all things: to whom be glory for ever. Amen." (Romans 11:33-

36)

There is no past or future with God, only the present.

"As there is nothing past in the consciousness of God, there can be no such act in Him as that of recalling the past to mind. He neither remembers nor forgets, in the literal sense, because the whole of His knowledge is simultaneously and perpetually present." [8]

"'Great is our Lord, and of great power: His understanding is infinite' (Ps. 147:5). God knows whatsoever has happened in the past in every part of His vast domains, and He is thoroughly acquainted with everything that now transpires throughout the entire universe. But He also is perfectly cognizant with every event, from the least to the greatest, that will happen in ages to come. God's knowledge of the future is as complete as His knowledge of the past and present, because the future depends entirely upon Himself." [9]

God had no need of being educated because He has always known everything.

"O Lord, thou hast searched me, and known me. Thou knowest my downsitting and mine uprising, thou understandest my thought afar off. Thou compassest my path and my lying down, and art acquainted with all my ways. For there is not a word in my tongue, but lo, O Lord, thou knowest it altogether. Such knowledge is too wonderful for me; it is high, I cannot attain unto it." (Psalms 139:1-4,6)

"Now unto the King, eternal, immortal, invisible, the only wise God, be honour and glory for ever and ever.

Amen." (Jude 25)

There is nothing that can begin to compare with the awesome, limitless, knowledge of God!

OMNIPRESENT

God is present everywhere at once. Although He is in Heaven, seated on His throne, His presence fills the Universe.

"Whither shall I go from thy spirit? or whither shall I flee from thy presence? If I ascend up into heaven, thou are there: if I make my bed in hell, behold, thou art there. If I take wings of the morning, and dwell in the uttermost parts of the sea; Even there shall thy hand lead me, and thy right hand shall hold me. If I say, Surely the darkness shall cover me; even the night shall be light about me." (Psalm 139:7-11)

"It is not quite correct to say that God is in all space. A. H. Strong remarks, 'God is not in space. It is more correct to say that space is in God.' Do not think of some invisible substance which extends from where you are to the farthest place you can imagine. The omnipresence of God must be seen in a spiritual sense. Since we are not bodiless spirits, it is hard for us to visualize what omnipresence means. The simplest thing to do is assent to the truth..., 'Do not I fill heaven and earth?' Jeremiah 23:24" [10]

OMNIPOTENT

The difference between the power of man and the power of God is that the power of man can only work with materials that already exist. The power of God is without limits and does not depend upon whether the materials exist or not. When God decided to create a place for the human race to inhabit, He made the world out of nothing. "By faith we understand that the worlds [during the successive ages] were framed (fashioned, put in order, and equipped for their intended purpose) by the word of God, so that what we see was not made out of things which are visible." (Hebrews 11:3, Amplified Bible)

It is one thing to create this huge planet out of nothing, but then God hung it on nothing! "He stretcheth out the north over the empty place, and hangeth the earth upon nothing." (Job 26:7)

And He accomplished all of this without becoming weary. "Hast thou not known? hast thou not heard, that the everlasting God, the Lord, the Creator of the ends of the earth, fainteth not, neither is weary? there is no searching of his understanding." (Isaiah 40:28)

After God created the earth as we know it in six days, He rested on the seventh. But the rest was not necessary because of weariness, but to demonstrate that His creative work had been completed.

Now, God effortlessly keeps His immense Universe running by just the power of His Word. "...and upholding all things by the word of his power..." (Hebrews 1:3) Is that not an awesome demonstration of the Omnipotent God in action?

Paul adds the footnote, "For by him were all things created, that are in heaven, and that are in the earth, visible and invisible, whether they be thrones, or dominions, or principalities or powers: all things were created by him, and for him: And he is before all things, and by him all things consist." (Col. 1:16,17)

The Crowning Act Of God's Creation

But the greatest demonstration of His Power was when His Son, Jesus, died for the sins of every human who has ever lived, was raised from the dead, and is now seated at the right hand of God the Father in Heaven, interceding for every person who will accept Him as their Lord and Savior. Every sinner who receives Christ experiences the forgiveness of all sin and is made a member of the family of God with full privileges!

"Revelation 19:6, 'The Lord God omnipotent reigneth,' is the only place in the Bible where one of the 'omni' words appears. The passage is part of a great voice of a great multitude which the Apostle John was privileged to hear in advance. For this marvelous sentence is part of a stirring chorus to be sung in the ages of eternity. George Frederick Handel has immortalized these words in what is doubtless the best-known masterpiece of classical religious music, 'The Messiah.' Recognizing the unmatched splendor of the famed 'Hallelujah Chorus' of 'The Messiah,' enraptured audiences traditionally stand during its performance. They have done so since its first performance. Could anyone do less when God's omnipotence is being praised so majestically?" [11]

IMMUTABLE/UNCHANGEABLE

God never changes. He is the same as He has always been and ever will be.

"There never was a time when He was not; there never will come a time when He shall cease to be. God has neither evolved, grown, nor improved. All that He is today, He has ever been, and ever will be. 'I am the Lord, I change not' (Mal. 3:6), is His own unqualified affirmation. He cannot change for the better, for He is already perfect; being perfect, He cannot change for the worse. Altogether unaffected by anything outside Himself, improvement or deterioration is impossible. He is perpetually the same. He only can say, "I AM THAT I AM' (Ex. 3:14). He is altogether uninfluenced by the flight of time. There is no wrinkle upon the brow of eternity. Therefore His power can never diminish, nor His glory ever fade." [12]

"Of old has thou laid the foundation of the earth: and the heavens are the work of thy hands. They shall perish, but thou shalt endure: yea, all of them shall wax old like a garment; as a vesture shalt thou change them, and they shall be changed: But thou art the same, and thy years shall have no end." (Psalms 102:25-27)

This characteristic of God helps bridge the gap that seems to stretch between the many scriptures in the Old Testament that appear to be at variance with the information which Jesus brought down to earth from Heaven about His Father. Jesus said that He is, "...the express image of his person..." (Heb. 1:3) The idea is that Jesus is the mirror image of God the Father just as the, "...exact expression or impression is formed when metal is pressed into a die or as a seal is pressed into wax." Jesus is the visible, tangible image of the invisible God. He is the complete revelation of God the Father to mankind. [13]

Interpretation Was Their Downfall

The Pharisees and the leaders of Israel based their concept of what the Messiah would be and do by what they thought they had read in the Old Testament. The fact that they interpreted what they read incorrectly is apparent to most today. But there was still enough information in the Old Testament, which seemed to support what they believed, to make a case for the kind of cruel, vindictive, blood-thirsty kind of messiah they came up with, to the point that they considered Jesus Christ to be an illegitimate, mentally ill, wine-drinking, liar who deserved to be crucified for blasphemy. That incredibly flawed, tragic, decision-making process alone should make every scholar of the Old Testament double and triple check their theories about what God the Father is really like, if they do not agree with what Jesus said about His Father and what He did while living on this earth.

God the Father cannot be one kind of Being in the Old Testament, and another different One in the New Testament. The unchangeableness of His very Nature obviates such an incorrect conclusion. "Every good gift and every perfect gift is from above, and cometh down from the Father of lights, with whom is no variableness, neither shadow of turning." (James 1:17)

Jesus did not kill anyone, or permit, allow or commission another person to hurt, kill or destroy anyone while He walked on this earth. On the contrary, He went out of His way to love, help, heal, and forgive the sins of those who came to Him with faith in His ability to do what He promised. He said His Father was Love, which will be covered later. He narrated the touching parable of the Father, representing His Heavenly Father, who welcomed back His prodigal son after he had wasted his life in riotous living, illustrating His Father's intense desire that every creature be saved. He promised Life to anyone who would receive it and revealed who actually was the one who does the stealing, killing and destroying. (John 10:10) Yet there still remains the tendency for some theologians and scholars, ministers and lay people to disregard the example and teachings of Jesus concerning His Father and choose the same, dangerous path which the Pharisees and Jewish religious leaders followed to eternal damnation!

HOLY/PURE

Holiness is the dominant attribute of God. Holiness basically is being separated from sin and dedicated to God.

"But I have said unto you, Ye shall inherit their land, and I will give it unto you to possess it, a land that floweth with milk and honey: I am the Lord your God, which have separated you from other people. Ye shall therefore put difference between clean beasts and unclean, and between unclean fowls and clean: and ye shall not make your souls abominable by beast, or by fowl, or by any manner of living thing that creepeth on the ground, which I have separated from you as unclean. And ye shall be holy unto me: for I the Lord am holy, and have severed you from other people, that ye should be mine." (Lev. 20:24-26)

On two occasions in the Bible the Holiness of God is

referred to three times consecutively, "Holy, holy, holy." (Isaiah 6:3; Revelation 4:8) On no occasion are any of God's other attributes referred to in this manner. No where do we hear the angels singing, "Life, life, life", or "Eternal, eternal, eternal", or "Love, love, love," or "Faithful, faithful, faithful". So it is apparent that the Holiness of God is a primary part of God's Character.

"God is called 'holy' more times than He is called 'Almighty.' It is not clearly set forth in Scripture that any one attribute of God exceeds another in importance. But without question the holiness of God is basic to all other attributes.

"What belongs to God is holy also. God's Word is holy. Romans 1:2 God's promise is holy. Psalm 105:42 God's Sabbath is holy. Isaiah 58:13 God's people are holy. Isaiah 62:12 God's dwelling place is holy. Isaiah 57:15 God's angels are holy. Revelation 14.10

"God is holy and His children are holy. But there is a difference. The holiness of God has no origin outside of Himself. Holiness for man consists in accepting God's holiness and obeying His commands. So God's holiness is original holiness, while man's is derived.

"In short, the holiness of God is His moral and ethical purity which sets the standard for holiness in man." [14]

"In the year that king Uzziah died I saw also the Lord sitting upon a throne, high and lifted up, and his train filled the temple. Above it stood the seraphims...And one cried unto another, and said, Holy, holy, holy, is the Lord of hosts: the whole earth is full of his glory. And the posts of the door moved at the voice of him that cried, and the house was filled with smoke." (Isa. 6:1-4)

"The creature should bow the knee in reverence before the Holy God. This humble recognition of the infinite distance between God and man is the 'fear of the Lord': that fear of the Lord which is the 'beginning of wisdom'. This is the expression of the feeling that we are wholly dependent upon God, and that He is in no way dependent upon us." [15]

Holiness Is An Inward Quality

The manner in which many Christians live today would lead one to believe that there is a general drawing away from the truth that God is Holy. It is difficult, at times, to even distinguish the difference between sinners and Christians by their way of life and actions. People, who call themselves "Christians", swear, lie, live in adultery, drink liquor, steal, tell dirty stories—in short, live like sinners— and yet believe they are in right relationship with God. But Eternity will reveal that they are only fooling themselves.

Holiness involves separation from this world's system and way of life. God's Word thunders out to the compromising Christian, "Follow peace with all men, and holiness, without which no man shall see the Lord." (Heb. 12:14) "But as he which hath called you is holy, so be ye holy in all manner of conversation; Because it is written, Be ye holy; for I am holy." (1 Pet. 1:15,16)

"Now the doings (practices) of the flesh are clear—obvious: they are immorality, impurity, indecency; Idolatry, sorcery, enmity, strife, jealousy, anger (ill temper), selfishness, divisions (dissensions), party spirit (factions, sects with peculiar opinions, heresies); Envy, drunkenness, carousing, and the like. I warn you beforehand, just as I did previously, that **those who do such things shall not inherit the king-**

dom of God.

"But the fruit of the (Holy) Spirit, [the work which His presence within accomplishes] —is love, joy (gladness), peace, patience (an even temper, forbearance), kindness, goodness (benevolence), faithfulness; (Meekness, humility) gentleness, self-control (self-restraint, continence), Against such things there is no law [that can bring a charge]. **And those who belong to Christ Jesus, the Messiah, have crucified the flesh—the Godless human nature—with its passions and appetites and desires.**" (Gal. 5:19-24, Amplified Bible)(Author's emphasis)

Not only does sin kill, but it will keep those who practice it out of Heaven, whether they call themselves Christians or not. The good news is that those who obey the Spirit of God and His Word have eternal life.

CHAPTER FIVE

JUSTICE/RIGHTEOUSNESS

In this chapter we will carefully examine the characteristic or attribute of the Justice of God. Many of God's misunderstood actions in the Old Testament can be resolved when this part of God's character is clearly understood.

What is the difference between holiness and righteousness? "Holiness is what God is...Righteousness is that nature, or character, in action." [1]

The Psalmist tells us that, "...righteousness and judgment are the habitation of his throne." (Ps. 97:2)

"God has instituted a moral government in the world, imposed just laws upon the creatures, and attached sanctions thereto. Because of the latter, he executes his laws through the bestowal of rewards and punishments. The distribution of rewards is called **remunerative justice.** Remunerative justice is based on divine love, not strict merit. The infliction of punishment is called **punitive justice**. It is the expression of divine wrath. God cannot make a law. establish a penalty, and then not follow through if the law is disobeyed. When the law is violated, punishment must be meted out, either personally or vicariously. In other words, justice demands punishment of the sinner, but it may also accept the vicarious sacrifice of another, as in the case of Christ. The righteousness of God is revealed in his punishing the wicked, vindicating his people from evildoers, forgiving the penitent of their sin, keeping promises made to his children, and rewarding the faithful." (author's emphasis) [2]

Moral And Natural Laws

The Laws of God have been established and set-in-motion in this world both in the moral aspect of mankind's conduct and in the natural laws of nature. By illustration, God has set the law of gravity into motion on this earth which automatically brings good or bad results to those who obey or disobey it. It is not a matter of God deciding what is going to happen or not happen in each separate incident involving gravity. The law of gravity is in place, operating regardless of what people believe about it or even if they know it exists or not.

The reason God set this law in motion was because it was necessary to prevent people from falling off the surface of this spinning planet and drifting off into space where there is no oxygen to breath. The law is a good law and the intention of the law is to benefit mankind, as are all of God's laws.

The law of gravity must be respected each time someone climbs a ladder. People who forget or arrogantly disregard the law of gravity sometimes pay with their life when they slip or fall off the ladder.

Or suppose a drug addict, high on some exotic concoction, decides he can fly, and jumps off the top floor of a fifty story building. In today's litigious society, that prefers to blame its every fault or problem on someone else, it is surprising that God isn't named as the cause of the drug addicts death. After all, he created the law of gravity, thereby creating a hazard for people who happen to think they can fly off buildings. (Appendix 2, p. 178)

Those who are aware of the Satan's activities know that it was his deception that caused the drug addict to take the drug and secondly, believe he could fly after the drug's effect robbed his brain of the ability to judge between reality and insanity.

Who then was to blame for the drug addict's death: God, Satan or the person who took the drug? Although Satan deceived the drug addict, it is the drug addict who is to blame because God holds each of us responsible for the choices we make. That is how it has been since Eve fell for Satan's lies in the Garden of Eden and then shared the fruit with Adam. Although Satan deceived Eve, she and Adam were still held responsible for the decision they made to disobey God's commandment.

In reality, God will send no one to Hell; they will go there because of the choices they made throughout their lifetime. God will merely hand down the sentence their disobedience of the Law demands.

"It would be unjust for God to set the law of gravity into motion and then allow it to work only for certain people. For a law to be just, it must be applied fairly to everyone. It would also be unjust for Jesus to die on the cross to pay the supreme price for the sins of mankind only to have His Father make exceptions for certain people. ...punitive justice is essential to God;"[3]

Sin Kills

The moral law of sin and death is one which sinners gnash their teeth on because they believe God is interfering unnecessarily in their lives with laws that take all their fun away. But the fact is that sin kills. Ask the alcoholic or cigarette smoker who has his life cut short by unnecessary habits. "The life span of an alcoholic is shortened by 10-12 years."[4]

Ask the AIDS victim who failed to obey correct biblical sexual behavior. (Although there are secondary victims who are innocently infected.)

Ask the people of India why they worship idols instead of the true God. India could easily feed its entire population, but because they believe the devil's deception and choose to believe a devilish religion that makes gods out of cows and rats, people starve and live in poverty because they cannot eat beef and the rats eat huge amounts of their grain.

Drunkenness is a worldwide practice that contributes to a great part of the misery in the world. Alcohol abuse goes hand and hand with poverty, disease, broken marriages, child abuse, spousal abuse, insanity, accidents, suicide and a host of other problems. But God does not force people to drink alcohol. In fact, He counsels them to avoid it as they would a venomous snake. "Look not thou upon the wine when it is red, when it giveth his colour in the cup, when it moveth itself aright. At the last it biteth like a serpent, and stingeth like an adder." (Prov. 23:31,32) Who then carries the responsibility for the evils of alcohol; God, Satan or man? Man, of course, for choosing to follow the deception of Satan instead of believing God's Word.

The demonic religions of this world are another trick of Satan to enslave mankind in rebellion against God and His Word. As a result, people who follow such satanic religious beliefs live in poverty, ignorance, demonic possession and spiritual darkness. They die of starvation, mothers throw their babies to the crocodiles to appease the demons or expose their babies in remote areas to die because they were unfortunate enough to be born as a girl or as twins or to have a physical defect. Is God to blame for their misery and spiritual death? No, the people are who choose to follow Satan. However, Christians will answer to God for the sinners they failed to reach with the Gospel of Jesus Christ, which would have given sinners the information they needed to at least make a choice between God's way and Satan's way.

Abortions kill not only millions of precious babies, which is hideous enough, but the secondary effects of abortion also have a serious impact on people's lives and even society. Who knows, for instance, what certain aborted babies would have contributed to society, medically, scientifically or socially, if their parents had not chosen to kill them within the supposed safety of their mother's womb. When the horror of what they have done dawns on some mothers, it drives them to dark fits of depression, fear and even suicide.

A Lie From Satan

Just listen to what Satan tells the mothers who believe the New Age explanation for abortion. "Your baby would not have been appreciated enough in this life, so by aborting him/her you have just given him/her another opportunity to come back again in another life to parents who will be able to provide for him/her those things you aren't able to supply." Satan neglects to mention that according to the myth of reincarnation the baby could also come back as an insect or alligator. But he doesn't care. All he wants to do is entangle them more firmly in his web of deceit.

The smoker receives emphysema, asthma, heart trouble and cancer. The drug addict; hepatitis, AIDS, malnutrition, crime, overdoses and suicide. The homosexual: hepatitis, AIDS, fear, perverseness and demon possession. Sinners have chosen to sin, so to be fair with them they must receive the wages they have worked so hard to earn—death. "For the wages of sin is death." (Rom. 6:23)

God Does Not Rejoice When Sinners Die

God takes no pleasure when people suffer the results of the law of sin and death. He says, "For I have no pleasure in the death of him that dieth, saith the Lord God: wherefore turn yourselves, and live ye." (Ezek. 18:32) Or this, "As I live, saith the Lord God, I have no pleasure in the death of the wicked; but that the wicked turn from his way and live:" (Ezek. 33:11)

"But doesn't God say in Proverbs 1:26, 'I also will laugh at your calamity?'

"No! The context of this passage begins in verse 20. It reads, 'Wisdom crieth without; she uttereth her voice in the streets...saying, How long, ye simple ones, will ye love simplicity?...' (verses 20-22) Wisdom is still speaking in verse 26, which reads, 'I also will laugh at your calamity...'

"It is wisdom—not God—that mocks the sinner. This passage is addressing those who cast aside all wisdom and mock its counsel. You see, there's a law involved—a fixed principle of God—that we call wisdom. If you cross the street when the light is red and are hit by a car, the wisdom present in that (traffic)light mocks your calamity.

"...His wisdom cries out to everyone...Those who should be hearing the voice of God—who instead are mocking that wisdom—will be mocked by wisdom on Judgment Day. At that time, wisdom will cry out, 'How foolish you've been!' 'Then they shall call unto me, but I will not answer; they shall seek me early, but they shall not find me.' (verse 28)

"Yet this same chapter in Proverbs also offers hope. It reveals God's heart in the final verse: 'But whosoever hearkenth unto me shall dwell safely, and shall be quiet from fear of evil.' (verse 33)"[5]

God's Gift Is Eternal Life

The positive side of God's Justice and Righteousness is that those who obey the Laws of God receive the positive results just as surely as the sinners receive the negative results. The second part of Romans 6:23 says, "...but the gift of God is eternal life through Jesus Christ our Lord." Believing the deception of the devil brings death, while faith in God brings eternal life. Mankind makes the choice; life or death? From that decision, justice is meted out according to which one is chosen. God abides by the free will He has given to mankind. Judgment rests upon the wicked who choose death, and everlasting life is given to those who choose Life.

There is much discussion, preaching and teaching about the fact that God is judging America today for its sins. But that cannot be true since there is no possible judgment of nations for sin until the middle of the Great Tribulation. (Rev. 14:7) Until then, God's plan is to reach every creature with the Gospel of Jesus Christ. (Mark 16:15) The final judgment for sin is the "Great White Throne Judgment" at the conclusion of the 1000 year millennial reign of Jesus. (Rev. 20:11-15) What we see going on in our time frame is the Law of sin and death in action.

These Are The End Times

"Now most would agree that we are approaching the end of the age, of which time Paul tells us, 'in the last days perilous times shall come...' and '...men shall wax worse and worse, deceiving, and being deceived.' (2 Tim. 3:1,13) Therefore, as man continues to turn away from the knowledge of God, the Almighty will continue to withdraw His hand of restraint, thereby giving man over to his own ways and the judgment that is contained therein.

"'And even as they did not like to retain God in their knowledge, God gave them over to a reprobate mind, to do those things which are not convenient (fitting, appropriate); being filled with all unrighteousness, fornication, wickedness, covetousness, maliciousness; full of envy, murder, debate, deceit, malignity; whisperers, backbiters, haters of God, despiteful, proud, boasters, inventors of evil things, disobedient to parents, without understanding, covenant breakers, know the judgment of God, that they which commit such things are worthy of death, not only do the same, but have pleasure in them that do them.' (Romans 1:28-32) This is why 'the wages of sin is death', for when man rejects God's Word, he judges and releases judgment (death) on himself."[6]

What about those people who have never heard the Gospel and therefore have not had an opportunity to make a choice between Life and Death. Paul reveals that Nature is a testimony of the fact that God exists. "For the invisible things of him from the creation of the world are clearly seen, being understood by the things that are made, even his eternal power and Godhead; so that they are without excuse." (Rom. 1:20)

Whether those who have never heard the Gospel follow up on that gentle nudge is the deciding point in what they choose. Testimonies abound of indigenous people who hungered to know a true and living God other than their dead idols. The Holy Spirit took that desire and, through a series of miraculous events, either led them to a Christian or the Christian was led to them to tell them about Jesus Christ, which led to their Salvation. Since God knows the heart of man, He knows those who truly desire to know Him, and He will move Heaven and earth to see that they are given the opportunity to choose. "Then hear thou in heaven thy dwelling place, and forgive, and do, and give to every man according to his ways, whose heart thou knowest; (for thou, even thou only, knowest the hearts of all the children of men;)" (1 Kings 8:39)

Law Of Life And Death In The Old Testament

In the Old Testament the moral law of life and death was also a reality. When the Israelites chose to obey God's precepts, they were rewarded with the peace and protection of God from their enemies. When they sinned and rejected God's counsel, death and destruction came upon them in the form of war and enslavement from their neighbors.

The part which Satan played in those events was obscure since there was little information in the Old Testament about what Satan did and his role in mankind's decision-making process. The name, "Satan" is only mentioned 19 times; the word, "Lucifer" only one time; the word, "devils" four times; and the word, "devil" is not mentioned at all. Does that mean that Satan and his demons were not around, killing, stealing and destroying in the Old Testament? No, their activity was hidden to the point that much demonic activity was actually attributed to God out of a lack of knowledge about such things.

The simple reason why God did not reveal more information about Satan at that time—who he is and what he does, in full detail— is because it would have unnecessarily frightened and frustrated the Israelites; they had not yet been given a means to control Satan. Not until Jesus came to earth and totally defeated Satan, stripping him of all his weapons, did mankind have a way of stopping Satan's activities. "[God] disarmed the principalities and powers that were ranged against us and made a bold display and public example of them, in triumphing over them in Him and in it [the cross]." (Col 2:15, Amplified Bible) "The reason the Son of God was made manifest (visible) was to undo (destroy, loosen, and dissolve) the works the devil [has done]." (1 John 3:8, Amplified Bible)

Until that victory took place, God instructed those who would listen, just as parents instruct their toddlers, "You have to trust me when I tell you that sin is bad and that it is something you must not do. You do not have the capacity yet to understand what the dangers are to your health, safety and very existence if you commit sin, so just take My Word for it and obey Me. **Stay away from sin**!"

God began the education of the human race about the dangers of sin with a series of covenants which basically said, "If you will obey me, these terrible things will not happen to you." Obedience was the shield God used to protect His people from Satan. Those who obeyed were safe.

Samuel later informed Saul, who had disobeyed the commands of God, "...to obey is better than sacrifice, and to harken than the fat of rams." (I Sam. 15:22) Obedience was preventive spiritual medicine that provided immunity from the deceptive virus of sin.

Those who placed their blind faith in God's Covenants and the Redeemer who was to come were protected from Satan under the shadow of the Almighty. That was the absolute bottom line protection in dealing with Satan during that time.

What A Change Jesus Made

When Jesus came to earth, however, that which was concealed in the Old Testament was revealed in the New Testament. Jesus revealed in John 10:10 that Satan's portfolio concerning the human race is to steal, kill and destroy.

On occasion in the Old Testament they were able to pierce the spirit realm and see what was actually taking place, as Exodus 12:23 demonstrates. The context of this passage revolves around the last plague in Egypt when any house that did not have the blood of a lamb sprinkled on the two side posts and the upper door post of the door suffered the death of the owner's first-born son and even the first-born of the animals. In verse 23 the events which would take place if the people obeyed God's instructions were described. "For the Lord will pass through to smite the Egyptians; and when he seeth the blood upon the lintel and on the two side posts, the Lord will pass over the door, and will not suffer the destroyer to come into the houses to smite you."

God Wasn't The Destroyer

The verse begins by saying that **God** would kill or smite the Egyptians who disobeyed His orders. But then the verse takes a 180 degree turn in the middle and concludes by saying that God would "pass over the door" and keep the **"destroyer"** from killing their first-born son.

Many have understood the destroyer to be a death angel of God that was under God's orders to kill the disobedient ones. Not only does this scripture not agree with that portrayal, but the revelation of Jesus concerning the Character of God will not permit that kind of conclusion either. Jesus names the "destroyer" as Satan, making the death angel one who was under **Satan's** command. (John 10:10) Not only did God not commission one of His angels to do the killing, but He was actually present to prohibit the death angel of Satan from attempting to kill **everyone**, whether they were the first-born son or not!

Another similar event occurred after the Israelites were delivered from Egypt. Many people believe that God judged the children of Israel for their sins when they failed to enter the Promised land, and then killed them in the desert as they wandered around in circles for 40 years. But Paul gives a different interpretation of what actually happened. The context of this passage is that people today should take note of what happened to the Israelites in the desert and make certain they do not repeat the same mistake. "Neither murmur ye, as some of them (Israelites) also murmured, and were destroyed of the destroyer." (1 Cor. 10:10) The real culprit in both accounts, the one who actually did the killing, was not God, but Satan, which fits the personality profile Jesus gave Satan.

A Life And Death Choice

God's Laws are set in place in this world. When humanity breaks the laws, they receive the result which is death. When they obey them, they receive Life. Indirectly, it can be said that God is responsible for what happens in people's lives because He set the laws into motion to begin with, but we have already seen that the one who breaks the law is the one who carries the responsibility for what he does. This can be observed throughout the Old Testament. God is said to have caused people to be killed, but in every case the people were killed because they had broken the Laws of God and were receiving the judgment for their sin.

An Important Truth About God

To understand God's actions in the Old Testament it is necessary to examine them in the context of the Law and what it demanded. **God always acts in a legal manner compatible with the Law**. That is why His actions are predictable when we understand the way the Law operates.

Under our system of Law today, a criminal found

guilty of murder by a jury in a court of law is sentenced by the judge, according to the laws of that state, to be executed for the crime against the State which he has committed. Notice that, although the criminal murdered a human being, the crime is considered to have been committed against the State because it is the State's laws that have been violated. (Of course the citizens of the State are those who actually constitute the State, and they have usually had some kind of imput into what the laws of the State will be.) The judge then pronounces the judgment or sentence against the convicted murderer, which the law of the State demands for the crime of murder.

The judge may pronounce the sentence, but he is not the one who actually carries out the sentence. That is done by the executioner. What is the difference between the killing that was done by the murderer and the killing that will be done by the executioner? The answer is that one killing was done **outside the Law**, in defiance of all the Law stands for, and the other will be done as **an arm of the Law** to complete the punitive action which justice demands for the crime of murder.

As an arm of the Law, the executioner is not guilty of murder and is therefore not subject to any punitive action on the part of the State. Nor is the judge guilty of murder since he is only applying the laws of the State to the crime.

Apply This Principle To The Old Testament

That is the scenario which is repeated over and over again in the Old Testament when God pronounced judgment on nations for the terrible sins they had committed. The big difference between our time and then is that instead of a single man acting as the executioner, as mentioned above, **the entire nation of Israel acted as national executioner,** as an arm of the Law of God, to complete the punitive action which the Justice of God demanded for the crimes the nations had committed.

What About Satan In All Of This?

Where does Satan fit into this legal setting? Does he also carry out executions for God? No, because Satan is an outlaw. His entire area of operation is outside the Law. In fact, he is the very reason there is a need for Law and Order in this world. Before Satan appeared in the Garden of Eden there was no need for an extended system of law. The only rule Adam and Eve had to keep was that they were not to eat of the tree of the knowledge of good and evil.

No one has any idea how long Adam and Eve lived in perfect harmony with God. There were no infractions of any kind; only peace and obedience. Then tragedy struck. Eve and then Adam partook of the fruit and were ejected from the Garden of Eden to separate them from the tree of Life.

God then established a system of Law to train His people or to act as a schoolmaster. "Now before the faith came, we were perpetually guarded under the Law, kept in custody in preparation for the faith that was destined to be revealed (unveiled, disclosed).

"So that the Law served [to us Jews] as our trainer [our guardian, our guide to Christ, to lead us] until Christ [came], that we might be justified (declared righteous, put in right standing with God) by and through faith.

"But now that the faith has come, we are no longer

under a trainer [the guardian of our childhood]. For in Christ Jesus you are all sons of God through faith." (Gal. 3:23-26, Amplified Bible)

For nearly 4000 years this system of Law was in effect. When God judged nations for their sins, executioners, who were arms of the Law, executed the law breakers. When the children of Israel entered the promised land, God's judgment was pronounced against the inhabitants of the land, the Hitites, Amorites, Canaanites, Perizzites, Hivites, and the Jebusites, because of their total moral depravity. For instance, "Archaeology reveals that the people of Canaan were involved in all kinds of idolatry, cult prostitution, violence, burning of children as sacrifices to their gods, and spiritism (cf. Deut. 12:31; 18:9-13)...The destruction of Canaanite cities and people demonstrates a basic principle of God's judgment: when a people's iniquity is full and overflows, God's mercy gives way to judgment (cf. Josh. 11:20)"[7]

Men, such as Samson, Gideon, Othniel, Ehud, Shamgar, and Barak, along with the armies of Israel, were the legal executioners of God's righteous judgment for sin, and as such were not held morally responsible for the bloodshed which resulted. Nor was God guilty for His actions as Judge because the penalty rendered was just and according to the Law. (see illustration l, p. 85)

Israel's Legal Position In The Old Testament

Because Israel was God's chosen, covenant people, they experienced Divine protection as long as they honored God's covenants. (Lev. 26:1-13; Deut. 28:1-14) When Israel sinned against God, their payment for sin was carried out in a different manner than the heathen's. When Israel

Law of Sin & Death

Romans 6:23

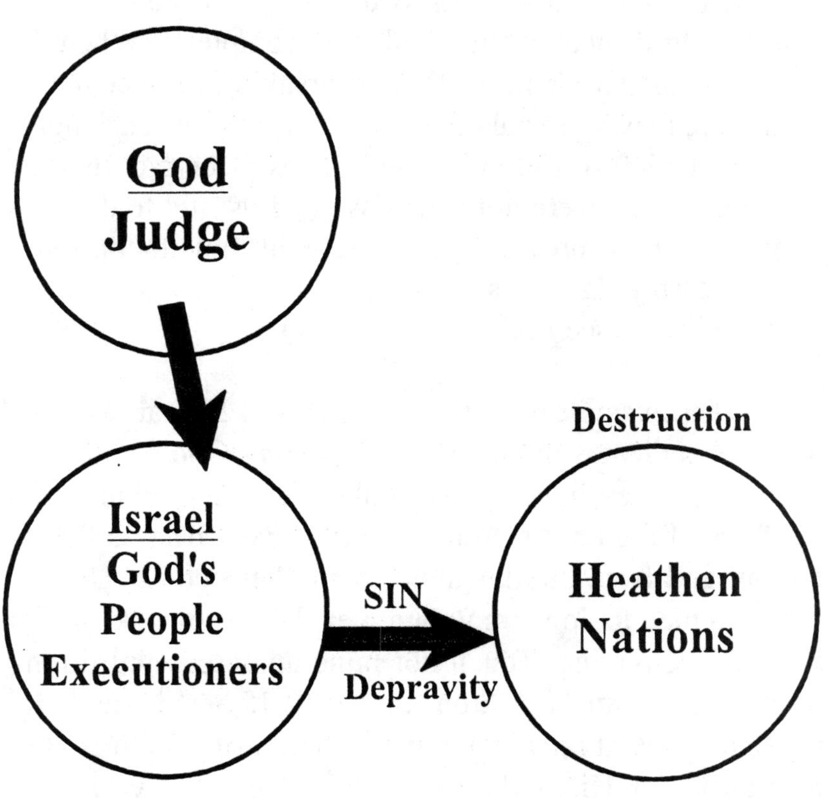

Justice of God
Sin demands punishment.

Illustration: 1

opened the door through sin, the heathen nations under Satan's direction swooped down upon them and stole, killed and destroyed, just as Jesus said would happen when Satan has a loophole in which to operate.

When God's people leave an opening or open door to the enemy, they allow him to do things to them that he couldn't do if their defense had been complete. When the Israelites lost God's protection by breaking their covenant with God, they were naked before the merciless onslaughts of the Satanicly-inspired heathen forces. The fact that the heathen nations were not commissioned of God to do what they did can be proven by the fact that they, themselves, were in turn judged at a later time for their crimes against the Israelites. (see illustration 2, p. 87)

The example of Samson, who served 20 years as judge in Israel indicates the danger of touching God's anointed, even when they have sinned, unless it is done within the confines of the Law. "And when they went from nation to nation, and from one kingdom to another people; He suffered no man to do them wrong: yea, he reproved kings for their sakes, Saying, Touch not mine anointed, and do my prophets no harm." (1 Chron. 16:20-22) If there is any judging to be done, it falls within the authority of God to do it or to men under His authority. "Judge not, that ye be not judged." (Matt. 7:1)

Samson The Executioner

Before Samson was born, "...the children of Israel did evil again in the sight of the Lord;" (Judges 13:1) As a result, God judged them for their sins and the Israelites were enslaved for 40 years by the Philistines. But the Philistines

Law of Sin & Death

Romans 6:23

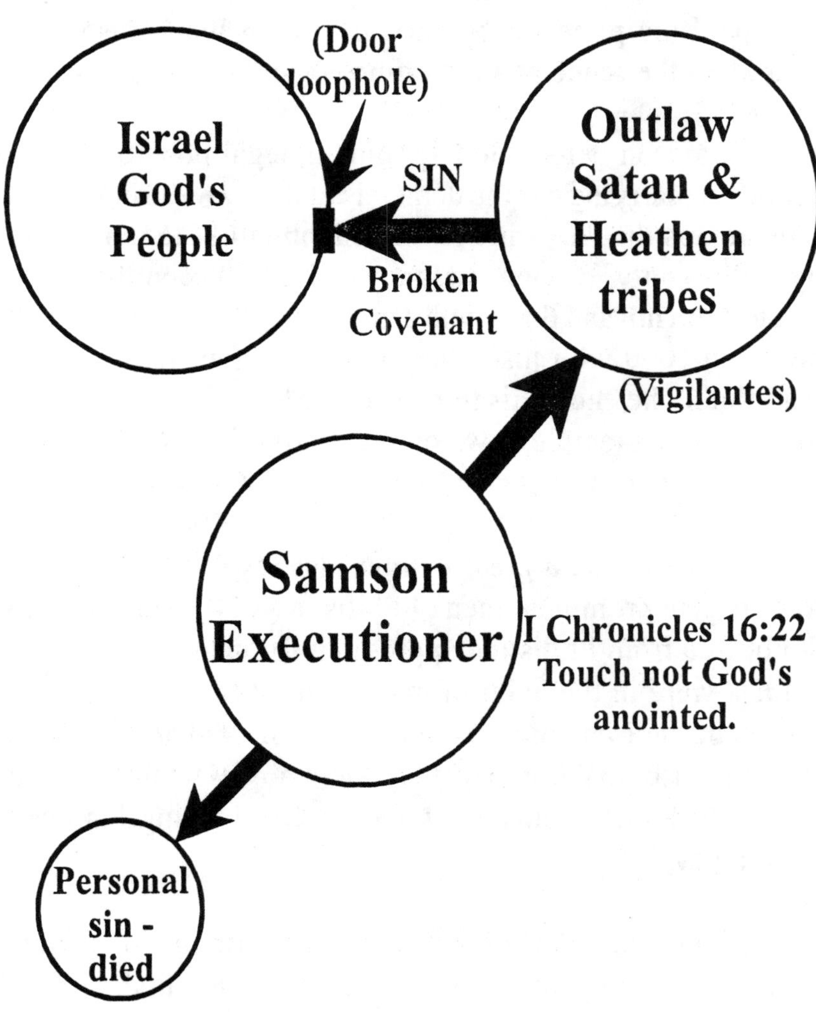

Illustration: 2

operated outside the Law. They had no covenant standing with God. Led by Satan, they were merely taking advantage of the fact that the "hedge" of God's protection was no longer in effect because of Israel's disobedience. They were doing what they had wanted to do for some time. They were not legal executioners because they were outlaws, and as such they paid the price for being vigilantes when Samson appeared on the scene at a later time.

Samson held a God-appointed, legal position as executioner, carrying out the demands of the Law during which time he was the Philistine's worst nightmare. He started out by killing only 30 men.. (Judges 14:19) Secondly, "...he smote them hip and thigh with a great slaughter." (15:8) Then he killed 1000 with just a new jawbone of an ass. (15:16) And finally he ended his time as judge by pulling the pillars of the heathen temple down on the heads of 3000 of the elite of the Philistines.

"With such a great number destroyed (of the lords, leaders, and prominent men of Philistia (v. 30) Israel was no doubt free from Philistine oppression for many years. Philistines were in the habit of making sport of even the dead bodies of their enemies, as in the case of Saul and his sons (1 Sam. 31:6-13); but now they were so defeated they did not try to hinder Samson's relatives from taking his dead body away." [8]

Samson, by his own choice, paid with his life for his infractions against the Law that he had committed personally, which points up the fact that no one is above the Law, no matter what position he may hold. But in his position as legal executioner under the Law, he was not held morally responsible for the Philistine's deaths because what he did was done as an arm of the Law. Nor was God, as Judge, guilty because He was carrying out the legal punitive punishment which the moral depravity of the Philistines required.

Outlaws Don't Carry Badges

Outlaws cannot function as an arm of the Law, as any vigilante group eventually discovers, no matter how noble their cause may be. They may hang a horse thief, which was the law of the Old West. But the mistake they make is to take the Law into their own hands instead of allowing the due process of the Law to function correctly, which includes a fair and impartial jury trial. For that mistake the vigilantes themselves were later tried and hung, even though hanging was the normal sentence for the crime of stealing horses at that time.

When Israel repented of their sins, God forgave them, reaffirmed His covenant (Dt. 4:25-31; 30;1-10; Isa. 11:10-16; Jer. 23:1-8; 30:1-31 and many others) and put them back once again under His Divine Protection which shut the door against any additional action Satan would have liked to initiate. As long as they kept their covenant agreement with God they experienced peace and protection in the land, just as believers are promised in the New Testament.

"We know [absolutely] that anyone born of God does not [deliberately and knowingly] practice committing sin, but the One Who was begotten of God carefully watches over and protects him [Christ's divine presence within him preserves him against the evil], and the wicked one does not lay hold (get a grip) on him or touch [him]." (I John 5:18, Amplified Bible)

When Jesus came to earth, died on the cross, and

rose from the dead, God took every one of Satan's "guns" or weapons away from him and has never given them back again.

Drop Your Guns, Satan!

"[God] disarmed the principalities and powers that were ranged against us and made a bold display and public example of them, in triumphing over them in Him and in it [the cross]." (Colossians 2:15, Amplified Bible)

Now, in the language of the Old West, believers, who accept Christ as their Savior and live according to God's Word which is the Law, become God's "deputies". Whenever Satan, the outlaw, tries to outflank the Law with some kind of deception, believers have the authority to bind him in the Name of Jesus, (Matt. 16:19, 18:18) or "throw him in jail" so that he is not able to accomplish what he would like to do in people's lives and in this world. *(See our book, "Strongman's His Name II," pages 87-90, for information on the validity of using Matthew 18:18 in this context.)*

"Behold, I give unto you power (authority) to tread on serpents and scorpions, and over all the power of the enemy: and nothing shall by any means hurt you." (Luke 10:19)

Jesus also took the keys of death and hell away from Satan (Rev. 1:18) so that now he can only kill people who, (1) do not know their rights as children of God, although God's Mercy fortunately protects them to a certain extent, (2) get into sin as children of God and do not repent, which opens doors or loopholes the devil can take advantage of to do damage, up to and including death, (3) are sinners and must accept whatever the devil decides to do to them, including death.

God's people, who live according to His Word, need not die in the manner that sinners do or according to Satan's timetable because Jesus now holds the keys of death. Death is but a release for believers into the next phase of eternity which Jesus has promised to those who live by faith in His Word.

"Jesus said unto her, I am the resurrection, and the life: he that believeth in me, though he were dead, yet shall he live: And whosoever liveth and believeth in me shall never die." (John 11:25,26)

King Jehosophat

The example of Jehosophat, king of Judah, (2 Chron. 20:1-28) is an Old Testament equivalent of 1 John 5:18 (cited above). Jehosophat had "...brought them (Judah) back unto the Lord God of their fathers." (1 Chron. 19:4) As a result, he and his nation were in right covenant standing with God and as such were under the shadow of the Almighty. Then the startling news arrived that the heathen nations of Ammon, Edom and Moab were about to invade the land of Judah. Their intentions were totally evil and Jehosophat knew that in the natural he and his people could not withstand their invasion.

Jehosophat immediately proclaimed a fast throughout the land and asked the help of the Lord. He went into the temple and, while all of Judah stood before the Lord, prayed a powerful prayer of only 224 words that swiftly outlined the situation as it stood. He affirmed the fact that

God had power that no one could withstand and that Judah desperately needed that help. In so many words, he took out the insurance policy and said, "We have met our side of the covenant, Lord, and we have confidence that you will do what You promised You would do in return.

God answered that prayer, as He always does with His covenant people, and told him, "Thus saith the Lord unto you, Be not afraid nor dismayed by reason of this great multitude; for the battle is not yours, but God's. Tomorrow go ye down against them:... Ye shall not need to fight in this battle: set yourselves, stand ye still, and see the salvation of the Lord..." (verses 15-17)

His instructions were not the usual kind of battle plans; they instructed Jehosophat to send the choir out to, "...praise the beauty of holiness, as they went out before the army." (v. 21) (Holiness is a powerful position of authority in God's eyes.) "...as soon as they began to sing and praise God He set ambushments (liers in wait) against the Moabites, Ammonites, and Edomites, and they were smitten (v.22). The ambushments were not of the Israelites so must have been angelic hosts. The Targum interprets them as angels. Evidently the angels of God appeared suddenly and the children of Ammon and Moab became so confused that they began to destroy the Edomites; then, after destroying them they were so confused they began destroying one another (v.23)."[9]

When Jehosophat, the choir and the army arrived at the scene, every enemy soldier was dead. All that was left for them to do was gather up the spoils of the heathen army, which took them three days to accomplish. (vs. 24,25)

It Pays To Be Faithful To God

The obvious conclusion is that it pays to walk within the structure of God's Law. The Moabites, Ammonites and Edomites were operating outside the Law, under the direction of the outlaw, Satan, so there was absolutely no way they could overcome people who had placed their faith and trust in God's protection which was their right as covenant people. Not only that, but God's people had a right to all the jewels and wealth of the heathen army of Satan. When Satan attacks covenant-protected people he not only gets trampled (Luke 10:19), but he also has to pay all the damages and "court costs"! **There is actually an umbrella of protection over those who place their faith in God and obey His Laws!** (see illustration 3, p. 94)

"He that dwelleth in the secret place of the most High shall abide under the shadow of the Almighty. I will say of the Lord, He is my refuge and my fortress: my God; in him will I trust. Surely he shall deliver thee from the snare of the fowler, and from the noisome pestilence. He shall cover thee with his feathers, and under his wings shalt thou trust: his truth shall be thy shield and buckler. Thou shall not be afraid for the terror by night; nor for the arrow that flieth by day; Nor for the pestilence that walketh in darkness; nor for the destruction that wasteth at noonday. A thousand shall fall at thy side, and ten thousand at thy right hand; but it shall not come nigh thee.

"Only with thine eyes shalt thou behold and see the reward of the wicked. Because thou hast made the Lord, which is my refuge, even the most High, thy habitation; There shall no evil befall thee, neither shall any plague come nigh thy dwelling. For he shall give his angels charge over thee,

The Law of Righteousness & Life

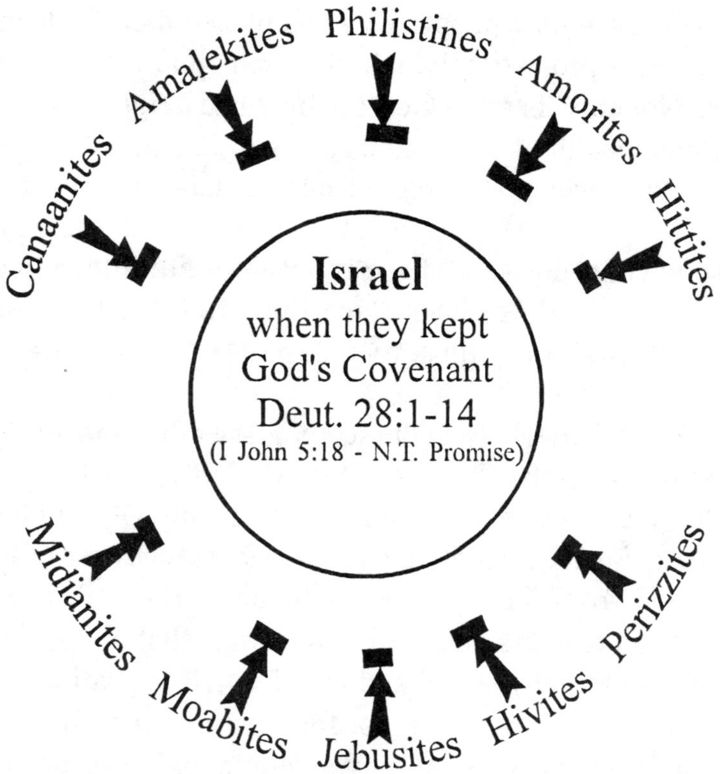

Israel's Enemies Could Not Touch Israel

Illustration: 3

to keep thee in all thy ways. They shall bear thee up in their hands, lest thou dash thy foot against a stone. Thou shalt tread upon the lion and adder: the young lion and the dragon shalt thou trample under feet. Because he hath set his love upon me, therefore will I deliver him: I will set him on high, because he hath known my name. He shall call upon me, and I will answer him: I will be with him in trouble; I will deliver him, and honour him. With long life will I satisfy him, and shew him my salvation." (Psalm 91)

The Other Side Of The Coin

On the negative side, King David got out from under the umbrella of God's protection when he committed adultery with Bathsheba and arranged for the death of her husband, Uriah the Hittite, to cover up his sin. Because of David's choices, God could do nothing but allow the consequences of his sin to take place because the covenant had been broken. True, David repented of his sin when Nathan the prophet confronted him, but the Law of sin and death had been put into motion. Nathan told David that his sin had been put away and that he would not die, but the suffering which his sin triggered was nearly unbearable.

God didn't cause his suffering or kill his baby by Bathsheba, although He was blamed for it by the Old Testament writer. Satan was the one who did it because he had a loophole of opportunity that he had not had previously. When David nullified the covenant, the enemy moved in to kill, steal and destroy, and the sword never did depart from his house. (2 Sam. 11,12)

True wisdom is to walk in obedience to God's Word.

CHAPTER SIX

GOOD

Jesus said an amazing thing to the young ruler, "Why do you call Me good? No one is good except God alone." (Mark 10:18) Jesus, the Son of God, who was with God the Father before coming to this earth, gave us His assessment of His Father's character that is irrefutable.

"The original Saxon meaning of our English word *God* is 'The Good.' God is not only the greatest of all beings, but the best. All the goodness there is in any creature has been imparted from the Creator, but God's goodness is underived, for it is the essence of His eternal nature.

"All that emanates from God—His decrees, His creation, His laws, His providences—cannot be otherwise than good: as it is written. 'And God saw everything that he had made, and, behold, it was very good.' (Gen. 1:31)." [1]

Jesus demonstrated that the reason He did good things was because His Father wanted Him to do them. "How God anointed Jesus of Nazareth with the Holy Ghost and with power: who went about doing good, and healing all that were oppressed by the devil; for God was with him." (Acts 10:38) This scripture shows that: (1) oppression comes from the devil. If it is God's desire that oppression be healed, then He could not possibly be the source or cause of it. (2) all three members of the Trinity, the Father, the Son and the Holy Spirit, were in agreement with the fact that Jesus was to do only "**good**" things.

"There is nothing but goodness in God, and nothing but goodness comes from him; there is no iniquity in him, nothing evil is his nature, no unrighteousness in any of his ways and works; he is light itself; all purity, holiness, truth, and goodness; and in him is no darkness at all, of sin, error, and ignorance, 1 John 1:5; nor does any thing that is evil come from him;" [2]

"The earth is full of the goodness of the Lord." (Psalm 33:5)

Sickness And Disease Kill, Steal And Destroy

It is amazing how some people can accept God as a good, loving God **until** they get to the matter of sickness and disease. Then all of a sudden He morphs into an ogre who plants diseases in His children like some kind of celestial mad scientist to make a spiritual statement in their life. **That kind of behavior does not fit God's character profile.** God is Good! Sickness and disease **rob** years from people's lives, money spent for medical treatment, and their quality of life before they die. That is the very opposite of what God wants for His children. Jesus came to **deliver** us from those kinds of things and give us Life in abundance!

Someone once asked Benny Hinn if he believed that God sometimes sends sickness to teach someone a lesson.

"No," he said, "how can a loving God who sent His Son to die and take away sin and sickness, one day change His mind and say, Jesus, you died to take away sin and sickness, but I'm going to send sickness to that young man over there because he needs to learn a lesson." [3]

When the man disagreed, saying he thought God sometimes sends sickness to discipline people, Pastor Hinn replied, "You know, my friend, I am a parent. But I would never think of striking my boy with a disease so I can discipline him. And my love for my boy is not to be compared with God's love for me." [4]

The man relented somewhat but said he still thought that God sometimes allowed it.

"Well, my friend," Pastor Hinn responded, "if you really believe that sickness is from God, if sickness ever comes your way, you should thank Him for it. If sickness is from God, why go to the doctor? If God sends you sickness, you might as well enjoy it! And don't take pills to get rid of it. Just keep it and let your body have a good time with it!" [5]

After Jesus cast the demons out of the Gadarene, He told him, "Go home to thy friends, and tell them how great things the Lord hath done for thee, and hath had compassion on thee." (Mark 5:19b) Jesus was concerned about the people's concept of God; what He was like and what He did. So He took time to tell them exactly Who had done this miracle and the reason why He had done it.

I remember when we were holding open-air, healing crusades in different countries of Latin America we had to instruct people who had only witnessed the "power" (slight-of-hand trickery) of the devil, "This is not something from the devil or anything like that, you are witnessing the Power of God as He heals these people. This is for real." How happy they were to learn that God's healings and miracles were permanent if they remained in obedience to God's Word.

The Gospel is not "bad" news—it's the Good News that God will do good things in people's life if they will believe, receive and follow what God's Word says.

The Goodness of God can be thought of as flowering out into four related petals: the Love of God, the Patience or Longsuffering of God, the Mercy of God and the Grace of God.

Let's consider each one of these petals of the Goodness of God which are an essential part of God's character.

LOVE

God is not just loving; He is the very personification of Love. Think of the most loving person you know or have known and that person will not begin to compare with the Love of God. "Beloved, let us love one another: for love is of God; and every one that loveth is born of God, and knoweth God. He that loveth not knoweth not God; for God is love." (1 John 4:7,8) "And we have known and believed the love that God hath to us. God is love; and he that dwelleth in love dwelleth in God, and God in him." (1 John 4:16)

Love is one of the major identifying marks to prove that people are truly children of God. "By this shall all men know that ye are my disciples, if ye have love one to another." (John 13:35) How sad that so few people in this world truly understand and know their Loving, Heavenly Father. So many think He is a cruel, unfeeling Being who is better left alone so that He won't give them an undeserved knot on the head from His club. But if God is really like that, why aren't his children taught to act like that also?

Do caring parents introduce their little children to God by telling them that God is cruel, unloving and uncaring? No, if they desire that their children have any kind of healthy relationship with God, they tell them that He is Good, Loving and Kind.

Are new converts told that God's children should do evil things to demonstrate the kind of God they serve, or are they told that they are to do good things? If it is true that God's children should do good things, why would God be any different? It would seem that the saying, "Like father, like son" should apply here.

1 Corinthians 13

The thirteenth chapter of First Corinthians paints an extensive picture of Love, and consequently defines God's Character because He is all these verses describe and more.

"Love endures long and is patient and kind; love never is envious nor boils over with jealousy; is not boastful or vainglorious, does not display itself haughtily. It is not conceited (arrogant and inflated with pride); it is not rude (unmannerly) and does not act unbecomingly. Love (God's love in us) does not insist on its own rights or its own way, for it is not self-seeking; it is not touchy or fretful or resentful; it takes no account of the evil done to it [it pays no attention to suffered wrong]. It does not rejoice at injustice and unrighteousness, but rejoices when right and truth prevail.

"Love bears up under anything and everything that comes, is ever ready to believe the best of every person, its hopes are fadeless under all circumstances and it endures everything [without weakening]. Love never fails [never fades out or becomes obsolete or comes to an end]. As for prophecy..., it will be fulfilled and pass away; as for tongues, they will be destroyed and cease; as for knowledge, it will pass away [it will lose its value and be superseded by truth]...And so faith, hope, love abide...but the greatest of these is love." (1 Cor. 13:4-8, Amplified Bible)

Love is best exemplified by what it does. Because of God's great love for mankind He gave of His greatest Treasure in Heaven to atone for their sins and bring them back once again into fellowship with Himself. "For God so loved the world, that he gave his only begotten Son, that whosoever believeth in him should not perish, but have everlasting life. For God sent not his Son into the world to condemn the world; but that the world through him might be saved." (John 3:16,17)

"In this was manifested the love of God toward us, because that God sent his only begotten Son into the world, that we might live through him. Herein is love, not that we loved God, but that he loved us, and sent his Son to be the propitiation for our sins." (1 John 4:9,10)

Does God Read Modern Child Psychology Books?

The fact that God is loving, however, does not indicate that He is "soft" in a sentimental, wishy-washy way, allowing His children to be incorrigible so as not to damage their little psyche. That would not be true love because love demands accountability. Loving correction signifies the presence, not the absence of love.

How then does God discipline His children? First of all, God does not use devilish methods to accomplish His purposes any more than human parents would copy the parental tactics of a child abuser to discipline their children. In this flawed world the Law still jails parents found guilty of abusing their offspring. God certainly would not be found guilty of actions humans cannot commit without suffering legal consequences. It is amazing that Christians would even begin to think that God is capable of doing evil things to His children which they would never consider doing to their own children.

What is the purpose of discipline? It is: (1) to stop the child from harming himself when he insists on doing something which he thinks is innocent and harmless, but which is actually dangerous to his health. (2) to teach the child the correct way to live so that he can enjoy life to the greatest degree possible. (3) to obtain positive results in his life. The parents desire that the child stop delving into negative activities for his own good and begin obeying the positive laws of God, nature and the beneficial laws of civilized society.

Can positive results be realized in child discipline by

using abusive, devilish methods? No, they certainly cannot!

"But don't you believe parents should spank their children? After all parents are instructed by the Bible, 'He that spareth his rod hateth his son: but he that loveth him chasteneth him betimes.'" (Proverbs 13:24) There is no doubt this biblical instruction is correct, but that does not give parents the right to use the rod to break their children's arms and legs or to kill them. That would never bring positive results. What good is that kind of discipline if the child dies? That isn't discipline, it is murder. But how many Christians believe God causes His children to have accidents which injure, maim or kill them, or puts terrible diseases in their bodies that cause terrible suffering and death, and then call it the "discipline" of God. No, that is not Godly discipline, that is devilish abuse.

Is This Biblical?

Amazingly enough, there is a teaching which has supposedly been adopted from methods used by shepherds in Bible days that supports the fact that even Jesus, the Good Shepherd, occasionally uses abusive tactics to teach us obedience.

It goes something like this. In the natural world of shepherding, when a lamb continually strays from the flock the shepherd breaks one of its legs and then carries the lamb around in a sling close to his heart until the bone heals. After that, because the lamb has learned to recognize the shepherd's scent or has developed some kind of close relationship through its close association with the shepherd, it will stay with the rest of the flock when it has recovered and never run away again.

It is true that Jesus compared Christians to sheep because of their unwise conduct, but it also must be remembered that sheep are not children of God—**people** are—and their is a world of difference in the way sheep and people are trained.

(1) It may be true that some shepherds break their lamb's legs, although I've never heard of such a thing. But if they do, they had better not let the animal rights people hear about it because that kind of shepherd could go to jail for animal abuse these days. Now let's just think about this for a moment. Are animal rights activists more loving toward animals, much less humans, than God? I think not!

(2) Of course this story is based upon the fact that only one lamb would ever need its leg broken at any one time. After all how many lambs could one shepherd carry around for months at a time if a whole group decided to stray at the same time? Five—ten—twenty? The most likely case would be that the rebellious lamb would lead a whole group of lambs into mischief who would all need their legs broken. That would tend to complicate the shepherd's leg-breaking activities.

(3) God does not infringe upon man's free will by using strong-arm, Mafia tactics to **force** His children to do something they do not wish to do, even though it would be in their best interests to do so.

(4) Jesus never once taught while He was on this earth that He would do such a cruel thing to His children for **any** reason. In the parable of the Ninety and Nine, nothing was mentioned about breaking the lost sheep's leg so it wouldn't get lost again. That would seem to have been the

appropriate time to mention such a brutal practice.

(5) There is no scripture in the Bible to support such a theory, unless it has to do with satanic activity. If any leg breaking is to be done, Satan is the one who does it because the sheep have strayed away from the sheepfold and are out from under the Shepherd's protection.

What Jesus **did** have to say about His sheep is that the Good Shepherd gives His life for His sheep. (John 10:11) "...and he calleth his own sheep by name, and leadeth them out. And when he putteth forth his own sheep, he goeth before them, and the sheep follow him: for they know his voice." (John 10:3,4) Jesus doesn't drive the sheep, He leads them. He doesn't break their legs to make them follow Him—they follow Him because they know his voice and choose to follow Him of their own free will.

Doesn't God Chastise His Children?

But what about the passage where Paul said, "My son, dispise not thou the chastening of the Lord, nor faint when thou art rebuked of him: For whom the Lord loveth he chasteneth, and scourgeth every son whom he receiveth. If ye endure chastening, God dealeth with you as with sons; for what son is he whom the father chasteneth not? But if ye be without chastisement, whereof all are partakers, then are ye bastards and not sons. Furthermore we have had fathers of our flesh which corrected us, and we gave them reverence: shall we not much rather be in subjection unto the Father of spirits, and live? For they verily for a few days chastened us after their own pleasure; but he for our profit, that we might be partakers of his holiness. Now no chastening for the present seemeth to be joyous, but grievous: nevertheless afterward it yieldeth the peaceable fruit of rightousness unto them which are exercised thereby." (Heb.

12:5-11)

The words, "chastening, chastisement, chaseneth, and chasened" in the above verses are used seven times. Possibly because of the old English connotation of the word chastise, more is read into the severity of these words than the original Greek meaning implied. "Chastise" conjures up the picture in many people's minds of an old English schoolmaster aggressively beating a barebacked schoolboy with a large, wide paddle. But the Greek word Paul uses in the above passage for "chastening" is the word, **paideia** which is the **very same word** he uses in Ephesians 6:4 for the word, **nurture**. That verse says, "And fathers, provoke not your children to wrath: but bring them up in the **nurture** and admonition of the Lord." Nuture is not a word that suggests harsh, cruel behavior. It implies careful, protective, intelligent treatment of something which is valuable until such time as it can survive on its own strength, such as a flower, a fawn or a baby bird.

Notice also some of the other descriptive words used in this Hebrew passage; "rebuked of him" and "corrected us." These are not violent terms which so many read into the intent of Paul in these verses. It is true that the word "scourgeth" carries a stronger meaning, but it is used just one time as opposed to nine other milder words or terms. The overall effect demonstrates that God's discipline is not cruel or excessive, but loving and firm.

When Paul encountered a situation in the Corinthian church where a Christian was living in gross, immoral sin and refused to repent, Paul didn't call down God's judgment on the wayward brother or even ask God to discipline him. He instructed the Christians, "...to deliver such an one unto Satan for the destruction of the flesh, that the spirit may be saved in the day of the Lord Jesus." (1 Cor. 5:5) When Paul wanted something done of a destructive nature in a Christian's life he delivered him over to the destroyer, to Satan, **because Satan is the one who does the devilish things to sinful Christians, not God!**

A Parable That Illustrates This Truth

The parable of the unmerciful servant demonstrates the truth that sin brings people under the dominion of Satan, or in this case, "the tormentors." Although Jesus was teaching Peter and the disciples on the necessity of forgiveness in the parable, the results of not forgiving are the same as any breakdown in obedience to God's Word.

Jesus told about a king with two servants. The first servant owed the king a huge amount of money. When the servant could not pay, the king commanded that the servant, his wife, and children and all that he owned, be sold and applied to the debt. The servant begged for patience on the part of the king, who was moved with compassion and forgave the entire debt.

The servant, who had received so much, then went out and found a fellow servant who owed him a paltry sum of money. He took him by the throat and demanded full payment of the debt. The poor servant did the same thing the first servant had done with the king. He fell down on his knees and begged for patience from the first servant. But it was to no avail. The first servant had him thrown in prison until he could pay the debt.

This was reported to the king, who then called the first servant before him and pointed out, "Shouldest not thou also have had compassion on thy fellow servant, even as I had pity on thee? And his Lord was wroth, and delivered him to the tormentors, till he should pay all that was due unto him. **So likewise shall my heavenly Father do also unto you,** if ye from your hearts forgive not every one his brother their trespasses." (Matt. 18:33-35) (author's emphasis)

Notice that the king did not do the tormenting, he turned the servant over to the tormentors. Neither is God involved in the tormenting of unrepentant Christians. When they choose to sin, they fall into the hands of Satan and are "wrung through the wringer" until such time as they realize their error, confess their sins, obey God and His Word once again and thereby come back under the Shadow of the Almighty.

What Is Godly Discipline?

Godly discipline begins in the disobedient Christian's life when the Holy Spirit speaks to him through God's Word, bringing conviction to his heart for the sin he has committed. Godly discipline is accomplished in the spirit realm, as the case is in any dealing God has with His children. (John 4:24; Rom. 8:16)

"Every Scripture is God-breathed (given by his inspiration) and profitable for instruction, for reproof and conviction of sin, for correction of error and discipline in obedience, [and] for training in righteousness (in holy living, in conformity to God's will in thought, purpose, and action). So that the man of God may be complete and proficient, well fitted and thoroughly equipped for every good work." (2 Tim. 3:16,17, Amplified Bible)

The Holy Spirit tells him, "You have sinned and that displeases me. Repent of your sin now if you want my continued blessing in your life."

In this condition, the sinful Christian progressively loses the peace of God in his heart and becomes miserable and unhappy if he continues disobeying the instructions of the Holy Spirit. Every preacher, guided by the Holy Spirit, seems to be informed of his particular problem and zeros in on it like they have radar.

This is a dangerous position to be in

The child of God is on dangerous ground here. If he does not confess his sin and obey the voice of the Holy Spirit, he moves out of God's perfect will for his life and into the permissive will where he loses God's total protection. (See illustration 4, p. 111) God does not desire that this happen. His Holy Spirit calls, warns and speaks to him, but God will not follow a wayward child when he wills to leave God's path for his life. Sin separates people who sin from God as surely as it did in the case of Adam and Eve.

The greatest punishment Jesus suffered on the cross for mankind's sin was not the physical pain of the nails in His hands and feet, the crown of thorns on His head, the stripes on His back, the intense thirst and the spear in His side. It was when He was spiritually separated from His Father by the sins of the world that He cried out in agony, "My God, my God, why hast thou forsaken me?" (Matt. 27:46) **That is the ultimate punishment God can inflict on His wayward children—separation from the greatest Friend they have ever had.**

Illustration: 4

Now the victim is naked before the onslaught of the destroyer who steals, kills and destroys. He is out from under the shadow of the Almighty. The hedge is down. As the disobedient Christian continues in the permissive will of God, negative circumstances begin happening in his life because the enemy has a foothold or open door that he didn't have before.

At this point, when the devil is tormenting them, many Christians believe it is God who is doing these horrible things to them—that this is God disciplining them. But that is not the case. God actually wants to deliver them from what is going on in their life if they will just come back to where they got sidetracked from His will for their life and repent of their sin.

We determine what Satan does in our life

Ephesians 4:27 warns that Christians are not to, "...give place to the devil." The good news is that if the devil has, "...no room or foothold...no opportunity...", he cannot do what he would like to do to the Christian. (Eph. 4:27, Amplified Bible) But if he does give the devil a place, he can do things to Christians he could not have done if he had not been given the opening or foothold through sin, the works of the flesh, ignorance, fear or even inherited weaknesses. Now the enemy can shoot his fiery darts of deception, lies, unbelief and temptation into the individual's life because there is no shield of faith to stop them.

This is not to imply that every Christian who suffers is disobeying God. The cause of suffering must be worked out between the individual and God. There are many reasons why Christians suffer and we are not the ones to judge which reason it might be. Countless people have been injured by Christians who "play holy spirit", telling everyone they are suffering because they have sin in their life. The only exception is when the correction is truly being accomplished through the Gifts of the Spirit, usually by those in leadership.

It is enough for most of us to just keep ourselves in sync with God's Word without horning into other Christian's lives. We must be sure that our own life is lined up with God's Word so that whatever happens is not caused by an open door the enemy is using to shoot in his fiery darts of deception, lies, unbelief and temptation.

Don't Cross The Line

At the point when the unrepentant Christian is defenseless in the face of Satan's attacks because of sin, the possibilities of falling away from God are very high if he continues to rebel against God.

There is never a good time to fall away from God, but this is a particularly dangerous time in history to stray from the truth because terrible deception is descending upon the earth at this time, just prior to the Rapture of the Church at the conclusion of the Age of Grace. "Let no man deceive you by any means: for that day shall not come, except there come a falling away first, and that man of sin be revealed, the son of perdition." (2 Thess. 2:3)

Simon Peter Gives An Example Of Godly Discipline

Jesus gave a first hand example of just how effective

Godly discipline can be shortly before He was crucified. At the last Passover Jesus celebrated with His disciples, he told Simon Peter that Satan desired to have him to sift as wheat. Jesus told him that He had prayed that his faith would not fail. Peter boasted (*the open door of pride*) that he was ready to go to prison or even die for Jesus if necessary. But Jesus ended the prophetic warning by telling Peter that he would deny that he even knew Jesus three times before the cock crowed that day. (Luke 22:31-34)

It happened just as Jesus said it would. Just before the cock crowed, Peter vehemently denied Jesus for the third time.

Now, what did Jesus do to discipline Peter so that he would repent of his sin and get back on track again? Did God strike him with a bolt of lightning to get his attention? Did a donkey cart suddenly roll down a hill, knock him down and injure him so he would have time to think of what he had done so he would get right with God again? Did a disease take hold of his body, causing him great pain, so that Peter would realize life was short and make his peace with God again? **This would have been a perfect time to do any or all of these things to teach the Church, which would soon come into existence, how God deals with Christians who sin.**

But all Jesus did to Peter was look at him! And although Peter was a rough, tough fisherman, he realized his sin and "...went out, and wept bitterly." (Luke 22:54-62)

How much more can Jesus accomplish in this regard now that the Holy Spirit dwells in our hearts. He can speak to us 24 hours a day, if necessary, to help us understand our need to repent and get back on our feet again. There is nothing like the "look" Jesus can give us through His Holy Spirit. Why would anyone believe it is necessary for God to use violence to get His children's attention? He says, "I will guide thee with mine eye." (Psalm 32:8)

The Compassion Of God

The Love of God also encompasses compassion which means, "to share feeling." "When Jesus saw teeming multitudes of people on a certain day, 'he was moved with compassion on them, because they fainted, and were scattered abroad, as sheep having no shepherd.' Matthew 9:36 'But thou, O Lord, art a God full of compassion, and gracious, longsuffering, and plenteous in mercy and truth.' Psalm 86:15 Though He is unchangeable, God is yet moved with deep inner concern for the people of this world. 'We have not an high priest which cannot be touched with the feeling of our infirmities.' Hebrews 4:15" [6]

God's Love Is Eternal

Finally, the Love of God is eternal. "The Lord hath appeared of old unto me, saying, Yea, I have loved thee with an everlasting love: therefore with lovingkindness have I drawn thee." (Jer. 31:3) Long after Satan, the false prophet, the antichrist and all sinners have been cast into the Lake of Fire because of their choice to ignore God's Goodness and Love, God will continue to love each and every one of them because His Love never ends. **He is love.** What a privilege it is to have such a loving, Heavenly Father!

PATIENT/LONGSUFFERING

Although some have difficulty distinguishing between

Patience and Mercy, there is nevertheless sufficient difference to merit mentioning.

"...mercy respects the creature as miserable, patience respects the creature as criminal; mercy pities him in his misery, and patience bears with the sin which engendered that misery..."[7]

"But thou, O Lord, art a God full of compassion, and gracious, longsuffering, and plenteous in mercy and truth." (Psalm 86:15)

"The Lord is gracious, and full of compassion; slow to anger, and of great mercy." (Psalm 145:8)

"The patience of God is that excellency which causes Him to sustain great injuries without immediately avenging Himself. Thus the Hebrew word for the divine longsuffering is rendered 'slow to anger'...God's wisdom and will is pleased to act with a stateliness and sobriety which becomes His exalted majesty." [8]

"...but thou art a God ready to pardon, gracious and merciful, slow to anger, and of great kindness..." (Neh. 9:7)

MERCY

"Not by works of righteousness which we have done, but according to His mercy He saved us," (Titus 3:5)

Mercy is the opposite of justice. In fact, mercy asks that justice be suspended because mercy characteristically desires to pardon the guilty. As we have seen previously, justice gives us what we deserve. If the Law demands death for those who murder, that is exactly what they receive—nothing more, nothing less. Mercy, on the other hand, seeks a way to treat the criminal in a way he doesn't deserve to be treated.

"Many people actually trust in justice and not in mercy. They say, 'God is just—God will do me no injustice.' True, God will do us no injustice. We need never fear that. But how terrible if God should do us strict justice! How fearful if we receive no mercy! If God does not show us infinite mercy, we are forever lost, as surely as we are sinners!" [9]

An Example Of God's Mercy

Jesus demonstrated the Mercy of God on many occasions. When the scribes and Pharisees brought a woman who had been caught in the act of committing adultery, they attempted to trap Jesus by quoting the Law's demand that she be stoned to death on the spot for her sin. They anticipated that Jesus would not want her killed, which indicates that these hard, religious leaders recognized Him as a merciful Person—a distinct weakness in their eyes. So they used what they considered to be a "character flaw" to give themselves the opportunity to stone not only the woman, but Jesus too, for not obeying the Law.

As usual, though, Jesus was three steps ahead of them. He didn't answer yes and He didn't answer no. He just stooped over and wrote on the ground. Finally He told them, "He that is without sin among you, let him first cast a stone at her." (John 8:7) The irony of this statement is that Jesus was the only one present that day who had the right to stone her because He was the only Sinless One qualified to carry out the Law's demands.

But Jesus used this setting to unveil one of the many sides of His Father's Character that He had come to reveal to humanity, the Mercy of God. True, the Justice of God and the Law of sin and death demanded that the woman pay for her sins. But Jesus was the perfect Sacrifice for the sins of the world who would flawlessly fulfill the Law of God to the very letter. He would pay the price for her sin of adultery with His own blood and thereby qualify, not to kill her, but to show her mercy and **forgive** her sins!

"When Jesus had lifted up himself, and saw none but the woman, he said unto her, Woman, where are those thine accusers? hath no man condemned thee? She said, No man, Lord. And Jesus said unto her, Neither do I condemn thee: go, and sin no more." (John 8:10,11) He didn't excuse her sins, He forgave them and told her she must not sin like that anymore.

This would have been another perfect occasion for Jesus to have said, "Woman, you need to learn a lesson from this. So I'm going to give you a cancer to teach you something. It will make you more holy and you will prove to me that you really love me by bearing this cross patiently. This will also be your 'Job's experience' so you can share in My suffering."

Why didn't Jesus do that on this occasion, or any other time for that matter while He was on this earth? The reason is because **God isn't the One who does those kinds of evil things—Satan is**. Jesus was demonstrating God's heart toward humanity. God doesn't desire that people suffer either in this life, or later on in Hell. He wants to save them from their sins and the results of sin. He wants to make them His children, give them eternal life, supply all their needs and care for them as any loving father wants to care for his children. The only condition He makes to mankind is simply what Jesus told the woman caught in the act of adultery, "Go, and sin no more." Why? Because sin kills.

God is Life—He wants to keep us alive!

What Happens When People Reject God's Mercy?

When people reject the Mercy of God and continue to break God's Laws, the outlaw, Satan, enters the picture through the loophole that gives him the opportunity to do things to them he could not have done if they had obeyed God's Laws. You really don't want to be at the mercy of Satan because he has none!

The Holy Spirit taught David Wilkerson a lesson about the Mercy of God that he has never forgotten.

"The Spirit said to me that night, 'David, do not ever accuse your heavenly Father of being less kind and merciful than you are as an earthly father. Think for a moment—there is no sin, no circumstance, no act of rebellion on the part of your children that would cause you to walk out on them. Even if they cried out to you from prison, you know you'd be there, with love and compassion. So, don't ever think your heavenly Father would ever be less considerate and caring toward you.'" [10]

Then he showed Rev. Wilkerson a vision when he was about to preach on a street corner in New York City.

The events in the vision were fictitious to illustrate the point God wanted to make. One of his children came up to him, who had sinned against him in a terrible way, had rejected all counsel and warnings and, as a result, was in deep trouble. But now he wanted to repent and begged for forgiveness.

In the vision Rev. Wilkerson turned away from his child and said that he had warned the child many times before and his warnings had been ignored. Now was the payback for sin and there was nothing else he could do for his child.

As he began to preach on the street corner, he told every kind of low-life bum, drug addict and murderer that God loved them and would show His Mercy to them if they would just ask Him to forgive their sins. He told them that there was no sin God would not forgive if they would just repent. Along with all the terrible sinners who came forward for Salvation, his own child also stepped forward.

This powerful vision illustrated to Rev. Wilkerson that just as he would not refuse the cry for mercy from his own children, God will not ignore our cries either. If God has love and compassion for every kind of mocking, evil, blaspheming sinner who humbles himself and asks for forgiveness, surely He will show mercy on us, His children, when we come to Him for help in our time of need.

Thank God for His tender mercies!

GRACE

Grace is unmerited favor. "For by grace are ye saved through faith; and that not of yourselves: it is the gift of

God. Not of works, lest any man should boast." (Eph. 2:8,9)

"Very often missionaries have found, when translating the Scriptures into native tongues of the heathen, they were unable to discover a word which in any way corresponds to the Bible word 'grace.' Grace is absent from all the great heathen religions—Brahmanism, Buddhism, Mohammedanism, Confucianism, Zoroastrianism. Even nature does not teach grace: break her laws and you must suffer the penalty.

"Consider a few contrasts between grace and the Law. The Law manifested what was in a man—sin; grace manifests what is in God—love, mercy. The Law speaks of what man must do for God; grace tells of what Christ has done for men. The Law demanded righteousness from men; grace brings righteousness to men. The Law brought out God to men; grace brings in men to God. The Law sentenced a living man to death; grace brings a dead man to life. The Law never had a missionary; the Gospel is to be preached to every creature. The Law makes known the will of God; grace reveals the heart of God!" [11]

"For the Law was given by Moses, but grace and truth came by Jesus Christ." (John 1:17) The Gospel gives us the Good News that Christ has satisfied all the requirements which the Law demanded for the punishment for sin. He became the perfect Sacrifice. Now any sinner who comes to Him and asks forgiveness for his sins is saved from his sins.

A Wacky Idea Concerning Grace

Paul takes up one aspect of Grace that has been abused over the years by a certain kind of people who always seem intent on taking Truth to an extreme. Their preposterous idea was that if Christians continued sinning they would be doing God a favor because He would then be able to pour out more grace on them.

To combat this error that had already begun circulating in the Church at that time, he asks the question, "What shall we say [to all this]? Are we to remain in sin in order that God's grace (favor and mercy) may multiply and overflow? Certainly not! How can we who died to sin live in it any longer?" (Rom. 6:1,2, Amplified Bible)

"The grace of God that bringeth salvation teaches us 'to live soberly, righteously, and godly in this present world' (Tit. 2:11,12) We are not saved by good works, but are saved unto good works—'Even so faith, if it have not works, is dead, being alone' (James 2:17); 'But put ye on the Lord Jesus Christ, and make not provision for the flesh, to fulfill the lusts thereof' (Rom. 13:14)." [12]

Grace is not to be abused, but received humbly and gratefully.

TRUTH/FAITHFULNESS

God never, ever lies. His Truthfulness and Integrity can be depended upon in all His dealings with mankind. "God is not a man, that he should lie; neither the son of man, that he should repent: hath he said, and shall he not do it? or hath he spoken, and shall he not make it good?" (Numbers 23:19)

"While most of us are quite familiar with faith, we may not be so familiar with the idea of faithfulness. The two concepts are closely related, but slightly different. Both faith and faithfulness spring from the same Hebrew root, *aman* (aleph-mem-nun). It is the same root from which we get our word 'amen.' Even the word 'amen' expresses the idea of God's faithfulness, since it means, 'verily,' 'it is steadfast,' or 'so be it.'" [13]

In a day in which truth is progressively becoming mutilated beyond recognition, it is refreshing to have a source of Truth that never fails. Possibly one reason people distrust God's Word is because their own word is not trustworthy.

"Sanctify them through thy truth: thy word is truth." (John 17:17) This is the basis of man's confidence in God. He is absolutely trustworthy, reliable, steadfast, stable, constant and true.

"Unlike all the pagan deities of past eras, God is not capricious. He is free from fickleness. He does not change his mind (Num. 23:19). He is a God who keeps His word forever (Isa. 40:8). He also keeps His promises with man."[14]

"Know therefore that the Lord thy God, he is God, the faithful God, which keepeth covenant and mercy with them that love him and keep his commandments to a thousand generations." (Deut. 7:9)

Can We Trust God With Our Life?

So many people have difficulty trusting God because they feel He cannot be relyed on for a variety of reasons. (*See Chapter I)* Consequently, they find it impossible to have a close relationship with God the Father because they believe that He will eventually take something from them that they value greatly just to see how they will react or to teach them something or to see if they really love Him.

But is God a Taker? No, the truth is that God is a Giver. The only things He takes from us are our sin and bondage and we are glad to give Him that.

"Never in the history of mankind has God taken anything from one of His children, except to bring something better, more beautiful, more fulfilling. God's best is not something to fear—it is always that which satisfies most. He not only knows what is best for you—He wants you to have His best!" [15]

God the Father is the most liberal giver in the Universe. He gave the greatest Gift He had in Heaven to save mankind from their sins, His Son Jesus Christ. And now, to those who will accept Him, He gives forgiveness of sins, adoption into the Family of God, eternal life, the presence of the Holy Spirit within, healing for the body, protection, happiness and joy, and every need supplied according to His riches in glory. God the Father never takes unfair advantage of anyone, in any facet of their life! Satan is the thief who robs and steals from us. (John 10:10)

When people understand Gods true Character, who He is and what He does, it removes the fear that at the moment they can least afford to be deserted, God will do something mean and cruel to them and then abandon them to fate. That will never happen to the child of God who is obedient to God and His Word. Deuteronomy 7:9, quoted above, is God's unconditional guarantee of that.

God Is The Only One We Can Trust With Our Life

Because God is faithful and true, mankind can have total confidence when they place their life in His hands. "And this is the confidence that we have in him, that, if we ask anything according to his will, he heareth us: And if we know that he hear us, whatsoever we ask, we know that we have the petitions that we desire of him." (1 John 5:14,15)

This must be balanced off with the conditions under which we receive the promises from God's Word. "Beloved, if our heart condemn us not, then have we confidence toward God. And whatsoever we ask, we receive of him, because we keep his commandments, and do those things that are pleasing in his sight." (1 John 3:21,22) Having a heart that doesn't "condemn us" is one that is free from sin.

"The sooner we trustfully resign ourselves, and all our affairs into God's hands, fully persuaded of His love and faithfulness, the sooner we will be satisfied with His providences and realize that 'He doeth all things well.'" [16]

LIFE

God isn't just alive, He **is** Life in the fullest, most expressive sense of the word. Life gushes out from God like a fountain, saturating the entire Universe with the vitality of His Life. Everything God touches comes to life. Jesus left the portals of Heaven to demonstrate the abundant Life which God is. "I am come that they might have life, and that they might have it more abundantly." (John 10:10)

How then can Life bring death? Did Jesus ever take

life from anyone when He walked on this earth? No, He didn't. Whenever He encountered death or the works of death, which are sickness and disease, He healed the sick and raised the dead. Jesus proved conclusively that His Father's desire is to **reverse** the death process the devil placed in motion through the sin of Adam and Eve, not encourage it, so that the human race can be freed from the process of death forever!

"Then answered Jesus and said unto them, Verily, verily I say unto you, The Son can do nothing of himself, but what he seeth the Father do: for what things soever he doeth, these also doeth the Son likewise. For the Father loveth the Son, and sheweth him all things that himself doeth: and he will shew him greater works than these, that ye may marvel. **For the Father raiseth up the dead, and quickeneth them**; even so the Son quickeneth whom he will." (John 5:19-21) (author's emphasis)

Everything Jesus did on this earth was because His Father was the initiating Force behind it! God the Father revealed His overwhelming desire to help the human race through the life and actions of His Son, Jesus Christ. That must be the focus when ascertaining who God is and what He does and that is also the basis upon which Scripture must be interpreted in order to arrive at Truth!

PROVIDENT

Whatever God creates, He takes care of. He does not create something and then ignore it when He becomes interested in other things. God didn't create the Universe and then forget it. He remains in vital contact with every infinitesimal detail of His creation.

"I will lift up mine eyes unto the hills, from whence cometh my help. My help cometh from the Lord, which made heaven and earth. He will not suffer thy foot to be moved: he that keepeth thee will not slumber. Behold, he that keepeth Israel shall neither slumber nor sleep. The Lord is thy keeper: The Lord is thy shade upon thy right hand. The sun shall not smite thee by day, nor the moon by night. The Lord shall preserve thee from all evil: he shall preserve thy soul. The Lord shall preserve thy going out and thy coming in from this time forth, and even for evermore." (Psalm 121:1-8)

"Preservation is God's continuous control of the created universe guaranteeing its ongoing operation. He sees to it that the laws by which the universe naturally operate remain intact. When necessary, He will suspend those laws and introduce a higher form of control—miracle. Government concerns more than the world of man and nations. The Bible is filled with the teaching that God holds the nations in His hand. Thus, by preserving nature and by governing men, God providentially rules the world.

"What are the objects of the providence of God?

"1. Physical nature. Job 38:28, Psalm 104:14, Matthew 5:45

"2. Animals. Psalm 104:21, 147:9, Matthew 10:29

"3. National affairs. Daniel 2:21, 4:32, Romans 13:1

"4. Chance circumstances. Proverbs 16:33, Jonah 1:7

"5. Tiny details. Matthew 10:30, 2 Kings 6:1-6

"6. Sinful acts of men. Genesis 50:20

"7. Lives of the righteous. Romans 8:28, Philippians 4:19, 1 Peter 5:7" [17]

"The earth and all the inhabitants thereof are dissolved: I bear up the pillars of it." (Psalm 75.3)

"Who being the brightness of his glory, and the express image of his person, and upholding all things by the word of his power, when he had by himself purged our sins, sat down on the right hand of the Majesty on high." (Heb. 1:3)

What a majestic, awesome God He is! He created the worlds out of materials that in turn had to be created. Then He hung the whole creation on nothing but the power of His Word. If God were to withdraw His support from the Universe, it would dissolve in a catastrophic flash of disassembled atoms.

Yes, you can be sure—God is caring for His creation!

ANGER/WRATH

God's Holiness and Justice demand that there be Godly Anger and Wrath. But notice that it is "Godly," not human or satanicly inspired anger and wrath. That reveals a great misconception about God and His Character. God's Anger and Wrath are not sinful in nature and are therefore not debilitating, harmful or evil.

Humans find it nearly impossible not to apply their human standards of conduct to God the Father. It is no more possible to understand the eternal, pure, Love of God in human terms than it is to understand His Anger and Wrath.

Unfortunately, humans try to do just that because they have no point of reference with God. He is in a category by Himself.

People sometimes stop loving each other and get divorced, which makes it difficult for them to believe God doesn't stop loving them when they do something wrong and "divorce" them. So instead of returning to God to receive forgiveness for their sin, they treat God as they would a divorced mate; thinking He never wants to have contact with them again. Christians also go for periods of time, thinking God is angry with them, afraid to approach Him for fear of rejection, when the only sane, intelligent thing for them to do is run as quickly as possible to God for cleansing from their sin.

Unfortunately, the fact that humans believe God loves them as they love each other carries over into their belief that God's Anger and Wrath operate in the same way as human anger and wrath.

This Is Not A Pretty Sight

What happens when humans get angry? Their heart starts beating rapidly, their face gets red, they scream and even lose control of themselves, striking out physically at the object of their anger, making statements they would never make under normal circumstances, making a complete fool of themselves.

But is that how God gets angry, or even worse, is that how God expresses His anger? Does He lose control of Himself as He screams out at sinners. Does He rant and rave as He sits high and lifted up on His Throne, with Jesus

Christ seated at His right hand and the Seraphims around Him saying, "Holy, Holy, Holy?" Does He fuss and fume and threaten to destroy people for not giving Him the respect He deserves? Does He say, "I've had it with those people! I'm going to wipe them out as an example to the rest of those imbeciles down there that no one messes with me and gets away with it?" Absolutely not! God **never** loses control of Himself for even a millisecond of time. He is the most balanced Personality in the Universe. **He is God, not a man!**

Possibly the terms "anger" and "wrath" are used in the Bible so that mankind can better relate to what God feels when He is displeased with their sin and disobedience.

Anger Isn't Always Sinful

Paul alludes to the fact that it is possible under certain circumstances for humans to have a kind of anger that is not sinful. "Be ye angry, and sin not: let not the sun go down upon your wrath:" (Eph. 4:26)

Jesus was angry in Mark 11:15 when He cleansed the Temple of the moneychangers. Apparently the **reason** for being angry is the key to whether it is sinful or not. Jesus was angry because of the sin which was taking place in His Father's House.

An important clue of what God's Anger consists of can be found in Mark 3:5. "And when he had looked round about on them with anger, **being grieved for the hardness of their heart**, he saith unto the man, Stretch forth thine hand. And he stretched it out: and his hand was restored whole as the other."(author's emphasis) The anger of God toward sin here is called "being grieved". It might be called a "white-hot sadness" over the fact that the people had followed the leading of Satan into sin instead of having compassion for the need of this man.

The fact that Jesus healed the man with the withered hand is further proof that His anger was not sinful, because God's Holy Spirit will not operate freely when sin dominates the situation.

What Is The Wrath Of God?

"The wrath of God is eternal detestation of all unrighteousness. It is the displeasure and indignation of divine equity against evil. It is the holiness of God stirred into activity against sin. It is the moving cause of that just sentence which He passes upon evil doers...Not that God's anger is a malignant and malicious retaliation, inflicting injury for the sake of it, or in return for injury received. No. While God will vindicate His dominion as the Governor of the universe, He will not be vindictive...We are prone to regard sin lightly, to gloss over its hideousness, to make excuses for it. But the more we study and ponder God's abhorrence of sin and His frightful vengeance upon it, the more likely we are to realize its heinousness...Each of us needs to be most prayerfully on guard against devising an image of God in our thoughts which is patterned after our own evil inclinations." [18]

The time when it appeared as though Moses was more godly than God after the golden calf incident should be put in perspective by considering the totality of God's Character.

"And the Lord said unto Moses...thy people, which thou broughtest out of the land of Egypt, have corrupted themselves...they have made them a molten calf, and have worshipped it, and have sacrificed thereunto...I have seen this people, and, behold, it is a stiffnecked people: Now therefore let me alone, that my wrath may wax hot against them, and that I may consume them...

"And Moses besought the Lord his God, and said, Lord, why doth thy wrath wax hot against these thy people, which thou hast brought out of the land of Egypt with great power, and with a mighty hand?

"Wherefore should the Egyptians speak, and say, For mischief did he bring them out, to slay them in the mountains, and to consume them from the face of the earth? Turn from thy fierce wrath, and repent of this evil against thy people...And the Lord repented of the evil which he thought to do unto his people." (Ex. 32:7-14)

It appears as though God is some kind of raving, unbalanced lunatic that Moses must somehow cool down to some semblance of sanity so that he can convince Him not to slaughter His own children. But how could a man be wiser, more in control, more loving and more merciful than God?

Something Is Wrong With This Picture

"In reading this passage, many Christians mistakenly attribute more grace and mercy to Moses than to God. They think, 'Moses is pleading for great mercy upon Israel, while God is ready to destroy them.'

"Nothing could be further from the truth! There was only one reason Moses could pray as he did here; It is because he knew God's heart of mercy!

"You see, God was speaking here out of His justice—and justice demanded that the people be consumed...So he pled, 'Lord, I know that Your justice is crying out, and You have to proclaim it. These stiff-necked people should be wiped out.

"But I know something else too, Lord. It's that You wouldn't be able to stand the pain if You did it!...

"The Bible says God 'repented'—which means, He changed His mind about how He would judge Israel. He wasn't going to destroy them. Instead, the people would waste away in the wilderness. Yet God never removed His mercy from them. Although the people would continue to pain His heart for thirty-eight more years with their unbelief, the Lord would still protect them, lead them, feed them and clothe them to their dying day." [19]

This episode involving Moses is much like that of Abraham when God told him to sacrifice Isaac. Moses knew God. He knew and understood His Character just as Abraham did. The psalmist confirmed that when he revealed, "He (God) made known his ways unto Moses, his acts unto the children of Israel." (Psalm 103:7) It is one thing to see the actions after the fact, but Moses knew the reasons **why** God acted as He did. It is always better to understand where someone is coming from when they do something, rather than have to try to decipher why they did it after its all over. To know God's Character is to know what His actions truly are, which in turn helps us to understand, as much as is possible in this vessel of clay, the reasons for His actions.

God Is A Jealous God

The Bible also mentions that God is a jealous God. But once again it is not the sinful kind of jealousy which humans have. On numerous occasions it is stated that God was provoked to jealousy. Deut. 32:16-1; 1 Kings 14:22 and Psalm 78:58.

However, Paul makes a distinction in 1 Corinthians 11:2 between human and Godly jealousy. "For I am jealous over you with a godly jealousy: for I have espoused you to one husband, that I may present you as a chaste virgin to Christ."

This is another example of the fact that God uses terms that mankind is familiar with to demonstrate His displeasure when His children are disobedient.

God never tells His children, "Do as I say, not as I do." He will not partake of sin after He has commanded us to stay away from it, of that we can be sure!

CHAPTER SEVEN

Satan's character is not a pretty sight. But it is necessary to take a brief look at it to know what a satanic or devilish action is, as opposed to a Godly action. Whenever any of the following areas of behavior are encountered by Christians, they can be absolutely certain they are dealing with Satan and his kingdom to one degree or another. On the other hand, they can also be certain that God is not involved in any way with these characteristics because God will never be involved with the satanic.

SATAN IS:

A LIAR — "Ye are of your father the devil, and the lusts of your father ye will do. He was a murderer from the beginning, and abode not in the truth, because there is no truth in him. When he speaketh a lie, he speaketh of his own: for he is a liar, and the father of it." (John 8:44) Wherever a lie is encountered, it is a certainty that Satan is involved because God never lies.

CUNNING — "Put on the whole armour of God, that ye may be able to stand against the wiles of the devil." (Eph. 6:11) All Satan has left to work with now are schemes and tricks. God took all his weapons away from him when Jesus died and rose from the dead. "[God] disarmed the principalities and powers that were ranged against us and made a bold display and public example of them, in triumphing over them in Him and in [the cross]." (Col. 2:15, Amplified Bible)

THE TEMPTER — "And when the tempter came to him, he said, If thou be the Son of God, command that these stones be made bread." (Matt. 4:3) God tempts no one. "Let no man say when he is tempted, I am tempted of God: for God cannot be tempted with evil, neither tempteth he any man:" (James 1:13)

DECEITFUL — "And the great dragon was cast out, that old serpent, called the Devil, and Satan, which deceiveth the whole world: he was cast out into the earth, and his angels were cast out with him." (Rev. 12:9) Only those who have and use the Truth of God's Word will be able to refute the deception of Satan. "But he (Jesus) answered (Satan) and said, It is written, Man shall not live by bread alone, but by every word that proceedeth out of the mouth of God." (Matt. 4:4)

A THIEF—A MURDERER—A DESTROYER — "The thief cometh not, but for to steal, and to kill, and to destroy:" (John 10:10) These characteristics are not found in God's Character. All earthquakes, floods, hurricanes, tidal waves, epidemics, famines—anything that kills and destroys—is a work of Satan, not God.

THE ADVERSARY—FIERCE—CRUEL — "Be sober, be vigilant; because your adversary the devil, as a roaring lion, walketh about, seeking whom he may devour:" (1 Peter 5:8) People and God are not the enemy—Satan is—so Christians should save their spiritual "bullets" to use on Satan.

WICKED — "Not as Cain, who was of that wicked one, and slew his brother." (1 John 3:12) Those who follow the "wicked one" do wicked things. Those who follow God do good, Godly things.

COWARDLY — "Submit yourselves therefore to God. Resist the devil, and he will flee from you." (James 4:7) This scripture goes together with 1 Peter 5:8 which says the devil goes about as a "...roaring lion..."seeking a prey. Some would call that "cruising" these days. But, for those Christians who know how to deal with him, the devil is not a lion and we are not his victims.

Peter knew something about the pedigree of this "lion". He is not really a lion at all to the child of faith; he just mimics a lion, pretends to be a lion, wishes he were a lion. Peter advises us to ignore what the lion looks like or sounds like and resist him, "...steadfast in the faith..." (1 Peter 5:9) We do it by faith because it isn't normal to resist a hungry, roaring lion in the natural. But when Christians, who are submitted to God, resist him, James promises that the lion will turn tail and run away from them as fast as his "legs" will carry him. **Satan is plain and simple a bully!**

We call his bluff by faith in the Word of God. So don't believe the smoke and noise and circumstances—believe God's Word!

REBELLIOUS — "How art thou fallen from heaven, O Lucifer, son of the morning! how art thou cut down to the ground, which didst weaken the nations! For thou hast said in thine heart...I will ascend above the heights of the clouds; I will be like the most High." (Isaiah 14:12,14) Lucifer, alias, Satan and the devil, is the biggest loser in the Universe. He is not very bright either because God has never lost a battle and never will. So who did he think he was anyhow?

A SOWER OF DISCORD — "Now the works of the flesh are manifest, which are these...variance..." (strife) (Gal. 5:19,20) Any discord in families, businesses, churches, cities, countries and the world is ultimately caused by Satan, no matter who is right and who is wrong. Satan just uses whatever available opening to stir up the mess.

PROUD — "For thou hast said in thine heart, I will ascend into heaven, I will exalt my throne above the stars of God: I will sit also upon the mount of the congregation, in the sides of the north." (Isaiah 14:13) What an ignorant, egotist. He has the least to be proud of than any other creature in the Universe.

AN OPPRESSOR — "How God anointed Jesus of Nazareth with the Holy Ghost and with power: who went about doing good, and healing all that were oppressed of the devil; for God was with him." (Acts 10:38) In this verse all three members of the Trinity are in agreement that God does good things and wants to free the oppressed from the oppression of the devil.

PERVERTED — "And said, O full of all subtilty and all mischief, thou child of the devil, thou enemy of all righteousness, wilt thou not cease to pervert the right ways of the Lord?" (Acts 13:10) Satan is the universal pervert. He is so twisted that he could not do anything straight if he tried.

TOTALLY EVIL—WITHOUT PRINCIPLES — Anyone with all of the above evil characteristics could only be totally evil. Satan is an outlaw who has no rules. He plays the end against the middle, or the middle against the end—it makes no difference to him as long as he succeeds with his evil plans. At this present time he is the prince of the power of the air, (Eph. 2:2) and the god of this world. (spelled with a little "g") (2 Cor. 4:4) He is the original source of evil in the Universe and his activities will only be ended when he is first of all cast into the bottomless pit for a thousand years after the Great Tribulation, and finally, into the Lake of Fire at the conclusion of the Millennium. (Rev. 20:3; 20:10)

By understanding what the quality of God's Character is and what Satan's sinister character is, the believer can sense immediately when he is being attacked by Satan and his demons or whether God is working positively in his life to help him become all that God knows he can be. Everything God does in people's hearts and lives is to make them better than they were before, while everything Satan does in people's lives is to drag them down to a lower level than they were before.

God and Satan never exchange characteristics. Satan will try to convince people that God is involved with evil, but he is not to be trusted. Believers must know who their Friend is and what they can expect Him to do according to the Promises of His Word, no matter what the situation may be. If they know God's Character, then Satan can't deceive them into believing that God can do evil things for whatever reason.

Satan Lost It All When He Fell

Many people, even Christians, believe Satan is a negative equivalent of God—the opposite pole from God, so to speak. The truth is that Satan is only a fallen angel. He is not even as powerful as a good angel. Where did people ever get the idea that when Lucifer fell into sin and lost his beauty, intelligence and position of power, that he became stronger? Does sin make anyone stronger? No, it doesn't. Sin invariably makes whatever it touches weaker and eventually kills it. (Rom. 6:23)

So where does the fable come from that Satan is this great, indestructible force—that, if we are fortunate, we just might win a battle over him once in awhile? I'll tell you where it came from—Satan's promotional department. The truth is that Satan is only a shadow of what he once was. Jesus defeated him so thoroughly that just the mention of His Name sends shivers through the kingdom of Satan. (James 2:19) Jesus said that we have **total, 100%** power and authority over Satan in His Name if we live righteously and act by faith in the Word of God. "Behold, I give unto you power (authority) to tread on serpents and scorpions, and over all the power of the enemy: and nothing shall by any means hurt you." (Luke 10:19)

Is This Strong?

In fact, to demonstrate that Satan is not as strong as one good angel, Revelation 20:1-3 says that it will require only one, good, ordinary angel, who is so nondescript that his name is not even mentioned, to toss Satan into the bottomless pit. And this regular, anonymous angel does it with only one arm because he is carrying a great chain and a key in the other hand! "And I saw an angel come down from heaven, having the key of the bottomless pit and a great chain in his hand. And he laid hold on the dragon, that old serpent, which is the Devil, and Satan, and bound him a thousand years, And cast him into the bottomless pit, and shut him up, and set a seal upon him..."

Does that sound like Satan is some kind of awesome, overpowering creature? Not if the individual has accepted Christ as His Savior, believes God's Word instead of the lies and tricks of Satan, is walking in the Truth of God's Word and takes authority over him in the Name of Jesus. "...in all these things we are more than conquerors through him that loved us." (Rom. 8:37) "Now thanks be unto God, which always causeth us to triumph in Christ..." (2 Cor. 2:14)

It is a different proposition if people get into the works of the flesh and sin. That is Satan's area of expertise because he invented Sin. He is a master at tricking the human race when people are away from the protecting influence of the Blood of Jesus and God's Word. Satan knows how to push all the buttons of mankind's flesh to present temptation in its most appealing light. Think how many thousands of years Satan has had to plan and scheme to match human nature with the depravities to which it is most vulnerable. He is a master in the hellish art of seducing people away from God and His Word if they don't understand what is going on.

Keep Satan Surrounded With The Word Of God

But when Satan is kept within the boundaries of what God's Word says about whatever the situation may be, he is helpless to accomplish his plans in people's lives. In the Name of Jesus the believer has total victory over Satan and his works of evil because Jesus has destroyed them. "For this purpose the Son of God was manifested, that he might destroy the works of the devil." (1 John 3:8)

And what are the "works" which Jesus destroyed? Some of them are: sin, sickness, fear, death, depression, oppression, obsession, poverty, anger, temptation, deception, lust, rebellion, discord and cruelty.

What a wonderful privilege it is to walk in the Truth that sets us free from anything and everything Satan would try to use to deceive and destroy us!

CHAPTER EIGHT

Not only is their a need to "...rightly divide the word of truth" in the **Old** Testament, but there are also areas in the New Testament that people have tried to misinterpret to correspond with the errors that have been made interpreting the Old Testament concerning what God does and does not do. The problem revolves mainly around Paul's epistles when he uses such words as, "affliction", "tribulation" and "suffering." A dangerous evolution in the meaning of these words has taken place, especially among those who believe that a downsizing of the Work of the Holy Spirit took place when the apostles died.

To match the Old Testament theory that God sometimes does evil things to His children, these people try to use the three terms mentioned above to prove basically the same thing in the New Testament: God "afflicts" his children with sickness or poverty to teach them some kind of lesson, or He sends "tribulations" to humble his children, or "sufferings" so that they can learn how to suffer for Christ.

But the Greek language does not support those allegations, nor does the Character of God, nor does the example of Jesus' life and ministry. But when entire denominations reject the fact that Divine healing is for today, they must find some way of giving sickness and suffering some kind of spiritual significance or benefit so that it will be accepted by members of their congregations as their cross to bear and thereby mask the fact that they have been robbed of part of the Atonement which Christ accomplished for them.

A Major Error In Interpretation

Paul's point in using these words was to encourage the Christians of his day to victoriously bear the **persecution** that was rampant at that time, as well as the persecution that broke out sporadically throughout the centuries that followed. The major error in interpretation is to lump persecution together with sickness, accidents and disasters. That is not correct as we will see in this chapter.

A Case In Point

"'Why is my mother dead?' 'Why did she have to suffer so?' 'Why do my children have to grow up without a doting grandmother?' 'Why does my elderly mother have to experience this grief?'

"Intellectually I could talk about and even accept all the commonly given reasons for it: Through suffering God builds my character and disciplines me. He teaches me to trust him and provides a counterpoint for joy. He draws me into the suffering of His Son and instructs me in comforting others who suffer." [1]

The author continues on with a list of other things God supposedly did in her life and family: more deaths in the family, unemployment and clinical depression, among other things.

Although it is not my desire to be insensitive, nevertheless it is necessary to authenticate that there are Christians who believe that this kind of thinking is not only correct but biblical. My desire is to point out in God's Word that thinking of this kind is a deception of Satan to keep Christians from receiving the full measure of God's Power in their lives.

To equate the things in the article with God's discipline is to accuse God of spiritual child abuse in the extreme. No human, Christian parent would withhold food and necessities, cause depression, grief, family problems and deaths in the family in order to discipline his/her own children just to build their character. Yet that is what God is accused of doing to His children by a significant segment of Christianity today.

If God were actually guilty of such actions in dealing with His children, then a case could be made that man's moral code of conduct is higher than God's. "Oh, but God can do what He wants to do because He is God," some would answer. But we have seen throughout this book that this is not true. God's Character will not allow Him to be involved in actions which are not God-like in nature.

Furthermore, it is not possible for Christians to be "...drawn into the suffering of His Son..." if the suffering the author is referring to are the stripes which Jesus bore for our healing and His death on the cross for our sins. That was something which only the perfect Lamb of God could do. When Jesus cried out on the cross, "It is finished," and died, that kind of suffering stopped and no one can take it up again and share it. "For Christ also hath once suffered for sins, the just for the unjust, that he might bring us to God..." (1 Pet. 3:18)

So what does Christian suffering consist of today?

"1. Persecutions for righteousness (Mt. 5:10;13:21; Mk. 10:30; Jn. 15:20)
2. Revilings and slander (Mt. 5:11-12; 10:25; 1 Pet. 4:4)
3. False accusations (Mt. 10:17-20)
4. Scourgings for [the cause] of Christ (Mt. 10:17)
5. Rejecting by men (Mt. 10:14)
6. Hatred by the world (Mt. 10:22; Jn. 15:18-21)
7. Hatred by relatives (Mat. 10:21-30)
8. Martyrdoms (Mt. 10:28; Acts 7:58)
9. Temptations (Lk. 8:13; Jas. 1:2-16)
10. Shame for His name (Acts 5:41)
11. Imprisonment (Acts 4:3; 5:18; 12:4)
12. Tribulations (Acts 14:22; 2 Th. 1:4)
13. Stonings (Acts 14:19; 2 Cor. 11:25)
14. Beatings (Acts 16:23; 2 Cor. 11:24-25)
15. Being a spectacle to men (1 Cor. 4:9)
16. Misunderstandings, necessities, defamation, and despisings (1 Cor. 4:9)
17. Troubles, afflictions, distresses, tumults, labours, watchings, fastings, and evil reports (2 Cor. 6:8-10; 11:26-28)
18. Reproaches (Heb. 13:13; 1 Pet. 4:14)

19. Trials (1 Pet. 1:7; 4:12)
20. Satanic opposition (Eph. 4:27; 6:12)
21. Groaning and travailing because of the curse (Rom. 8:17-26)"[2]

With the exception of number 21, all of the above sufferings are entirely related to persecution for the cause of Christ. That should not be surprising because Jesus told his disciples, "Remember the word that I said unto you, The servant is not greater than his lord. If they have persecuted me, they will also persecute you." (John 15:20) Note that Jesus did not tell his disciples that they would have to go through sickness and disease. Why not? Because He paid the price so that they would not have to suffer sickness and disease again, "...by whose stripes ye were healed." (1 Pet. 2:24)

Therefore persecution should be a normal part of the Christian's life, but not sickness and disease, provided the believer appropriates what Christ accomplished for him. Jesus did not take the stripes on His back to keep believers from being persecuted, but He did to heal their bodies.

Christ Is Our Example Of How Believers Should Suffer Persecution.

"For even hereunto were ye called: because Christ also suffered for us, leaving an example, that ye should follow his steps. Who did no sin, neither was guile found in his mouth: Who, when he was reviled, reviled not again; when he suffered, he threatened not; but committed himself to him that judgeth righteously." (1 Pet. 2:21-23)

There is also some confusion over the passage in

Hebrews 5:8,9. "Though he were a Son, yet learned he obedience by the things which he suffered. And being made perfect, he became the author of eternal salvation unto all them that obey him."

One of the reasons there is a problem with the word "suffering" in some parts of the Christian community is because there has been very little religious persecution in the United States compared to the rest of the world. People who accept Christ in the Muslim world, however, have no difficulty understanding that "suffering" for Christ can mean something other than sickness. Many of them are killed for their testimony with the full blessing of the Muslim religion.

During our service as missionaries in Costa Rica, a close friend told me that when he accepted Christ his mother told him, "You are no longer my son." For eight, long years he suffered the loss of his family until his mother also accepted Christ. Another Costa Rican told me, "My family told me that they would rather that I be an alcoholic than an Evangelical Christian." That is suffering for Christ!

There is a concerted effort in our culture today to single out the Christian faith as "extreme". New Agers have clearly written that they plan to eliminate the Christians and the Jews when they take over the world. Should Jesus tarry it could well be that we will learn about that side of "suffering" here in the United States before we are done with this earthly life.

In the case of Jesus learning obedience by the things He suffered, it is a simple matter of considering the persecution He suffered. Paul details what happened when Jesus came to earth from Heaven. He, "...stripped Himself [of all privileges and rightful dignity] so as to assume the guise of a servant (slave), in that He became like men and was born a human being." (Phil. 2:7, Amplified Bible)

We may not think that is such a great sacrifice, but look at it from the viewpoint of Jesus. He had to leave the power, glory and adoration that was His in Heaven and come down to this rotten world, be born in a stable and have to suffer temptation like everyone else. "For in that he himself hath suffered being tempted, he is able to succour them that are tempted." (Heb. 2:18)

Imagine Diaper-Training The Son Of God!

He suffered the indignity of being a baby, having to learn rules of human behavior and how to deal with the thousand and one idiosyncrasies of human life. After He began His ministry He was tempted in the desert for 40 days and nights. Then He was hounded by the scribes and Pharisees like a criminal. Even His own family thought He was having a breakdown of some kind. Non-constructive criticism from those who are close to us, because we are following the will of God, can be a devastating form of persecution.

The key phrase in judging whether the persecution we suffer is for the Kingdom of God can be found in these words of Jesus. "Blessed are they which are persecuted for **righteousness' sake**: for their's is the kingdom of heaven." (Matt. 5:10)(author's emphasis) Being persecuted because we do something dumb or for being a "smart mouth" is not persecution "for righteousness sake."

Can you not sense the atmosphere of persecution for

righteousness' sake in this scripture? "...Love your enemies, bless them that curse you, do good to them that hate you, and pray for them which despitefully use you, and persecute you:" (Matt. 5:44)

Religious Persecution

Persecution for righteousness sake can also come from the religious world. The religious element of Jesus' day were those who perpetrated the crucifixion of Jesus. Pilate, **a sinner**, wanted to free Jesus, but the "religious" Pharisees incited the people to yell, "Crucify Him." The Pharisees had rejected the truth of God's Word and, as a result, had lost their scriptural point of reference. That spirit is still active in the religious world today and will bring us the same opportunities to suffer persecution for righteousness sake, if we displease them, as it did for Jesus nearly 2000 years ago.

"...the greatest, most ferocious persecution against God's holy remnant comes from religious leaders and their followers who reject the offense of the Cross of Christ. All persecution of God's people centers on the Cross. Paul said, 'As many as desire to make a fair show in the flesh, they constrain you to be circumcised; only LEST THEY SHOULD SUFFER PERSECUTION FOR THE CROSS OF CHRIST...' (Galatians 6:12)

"Paul said, 'If I preach circumcision, why do I yet suffer persecution? Then is the offense of the Cross ceased.' (Galations 5:11) In other words...You can enjoy the fellowship and good will of the entire religious system if you will simply conform to all their bland, lifeless, middle-of-the-road standards." [3]

An examination of the original Greek meanings of the words Paul used when he talked about tribulation, affliction and suffering demonstrates the disservice perpetrated on the Body of Christ by the teaching of those who believe that God uses devilish actions to teach and discipline His children.

"Thlipsis" "This Greek word is translated in the King James version as, 'tribulation' 20 times, and 'affliction in the sense of persecution' 18 times. It is also translated, 'burdened' in 2 Corinthians 8:13, 'anguished' in John 16:21, and 'troubled' in 1 Corinthians 7:28 and 2 Corinthians 1:4,8. **Not one time is 'thlipsis' used for physical sickness or disease!"**[4]

Here are five scriptures where **"thlipsis"** was translated as "tribulation" and "affliction", but had no connection to sickness and disease.

1. 2 CORINTHIANS 1:4 — "Who comforteth us in all *tribulation,* **(thlipsis)** that we may be able to comfort them which are in any trouble, by the comfort wherewith we ourselves are comforted of God."

Paul says that when God comforts them in their persecution, they will be able, in turn, to use the comfort which God has given them to comfort others who are being persecuted.

2. HEBREWS 10:33,34 — "Partly, whilst ye were made a gazingstock both by reproaches and *afflictions* **(thlipsis)**;...For ye had compassion of me in my bonds..."

Paul was a prisoner, not sick!

3. 1 THESSALONIANS 3:3 — "That no man should be moved by these *afflictions*:"**(thlipsis)**

That was the affliction of being a prisoner in prison which could be a nightmare in those days.

4. PHILIPPIANS 4:13,14 — "I can do all things through Christ which strengtheneth me. Notwithstanding ye have well done that ye did communicate with my *afflictions*."**(thlipsis)**

Prison once again. He was in prison for his testimony of Jesus Christ.

5. 1 THESSALONIANS 1:6 — "And ye became followers of us, and of the Lord, having received the word in much *affliction*, **(thlipsis)** with joy of the Holy Ghost."

Those who believe Paul was talking about sickness in these verses have missed what Paul was saying. He was demonstrating that persecution is a normal part of the Christian life. "Why is that?" Because persecution "divides the men from the boys," spiritually speaking. It makes those Christians stronger who have their life rooted in the Word of God, and additionally, it is a tremendous testimony of the power of God to the unsaved world. It also weeds out those who have a faulty root system.

"But he that received the seed into stony places, the same is he that heareth the word, and anon with joy receiveth it; Yet hath he not root in himself, but endureth for a while: for when *tribulation* **(thlipsis)** or persecution ariseth because of the word, by and by he is offended." (Matt. 13:20,21)

("...at once he is caused to stumble [he is repelled and begins to distrust and desert Him Whom he ought to trust and obey] and he falls away." (Matt. 13:21b Amplified Bible)

"Beloved, think it not strange concerning the fiery trial * which is to try you, as though some strange thing happened unto you: but rejoice, inasmuch as ye are partakers of Christ's sufferings;* that, when his glory shall be revealed, ye may be glad also with exceeding joy." (1 Pet. 4:12,13)

*1. "fiery trial" is the same Greek word as the word, "trial of your faith" in 1 Peter 1:7, which is "dokimion", Strong's Concordance word number 1383, which means, "a testing", by implication "trustworthiness" of faith.

*2 See listing of 21 kinds of suffering Christians suffer for Christ.

Here are other Greek words that have been misinterpreted to mean "sickness and accidents" when they actually should carry the meaning of "persecution."

"Thlibo"—means to suffer tribulation, trouble. [5]

"And whether we be *afflicted*, **(thlibo)** it is for your consolation and salvation, which is effectual in the enduring of the same *sufferings* (**"pathema"** persecution) which we also suffer." (2 Cor. 1:6) [6]

The idea here was that the persecution which Paul endured was good because it gave his fellow Christians an example of how they were, in turn, to handle persecution when it came their way.

"Sugkowcheo"—means to endure ill-treatment,

wrong, hurt or injury. [7]

"Choosing rather to suffer *affliction* with the people of God, than to enjoy the pleasures of sin for a season;" (Heb. 11:25)

"Astheneia"—has reference to weakness, not from disease. [8]

For instance, the crucifixion appeared to be Christ's weakness and defeat to the people of that day. He seemed totally powerless to overcome it. But out of that apparent defeat, His power was demonstrated. His followers today are also weak, which causes them to cleave to Christ, and that very weakness brings them life and power.

"My grace is sufficient for thee: for my strength is made perfect in weakness. Most gladly therefore will I rather glory in my *infirmities*, (**astheneia**) that the power of Christ may rest upon me." (2 Cor. 12:9)

Paul's Thorn In The Flesh Explained

Paul's thorn in the flesh was not sickness, but persecution, which had to do with the trials, troubles and sufferings he listed in 2 Corinthians 11:24-29, "Of the Jews five times received I forty stripes save one. Thrice was I beaten with rods, once was I stoned, thrice I suffered shipwreck, a night and a day I have been in the deep; in journeyings often, in perils of waters, in perils of robbers, in perils by mine own countrymen, in perils by the heathen, in perils in the city, in perils in the wilderness, in perils in the sea, in perils among false brethren, in weariness and painfulness, in watchings often, in hunger and thirst, in fastings often, in cold and nakedness. Besides those things that are without, that which cometh upon me daily, the care of all the churches. Who is weak, and I am not weak? who is offended, and I burn not?"

Then he reveals **why** the "thorn in the flesh" was given to him with his own words, "And lest I should be exalted above measure through the abundance of the revelations, there was given to me a thorn in the flesh, the messenger of Satan to buffet me, lest I should be exalted above measure." (2 Cor. 12:7)

Paul Had Spiritual Problems Like Everyone

It is significant that Paul begins and ends this verse with the same, exact words, "...lest I should be exalted above measure..." Paul was not perfect. In our way of speaking today he was saying, "So I wouldn't have pride because of the great number of tremendous revelations I received from God..." He, himself, admits he had a problem with pride and **that** was the reason the thorn in the flesh was given to him. Many theologians assume this was a sickness or bad eyesight, but that is only conjecture—they have no proof of that in the context of the scripture.

"Paul's thorn must be understood in the same sense as Num. 33:55; Ezek. 28:24; Hos. 2:6 where the same Greek (word) *skolop*, thorn, is found in the Septuigent. Were those giants and enemies of Israel diseases in their sides or the cause of their wars and other kinds of sufferings?" [9]

In other words, Israel's problems were not sickness and diseases, but the armies of their enemies who ran roughshod over them. In today's speech people would say that "so and so is a pain in the neck to me", instead of "a thorn in the flesh", to signify that someone is bothering or tormenting them.

The Thorn Was From Satan

Finally, Paul tells us **who** it was that sent the thorn in the flesh. It was, "...a messenger of Satan..." How could theologians believe that God gave this to Paul when the verse plainly says it was from Satan? God doesn't use Satan's messengers, evil spirits, to do His work for Him. He has His Holy Spirit to accomplish His will.

What did this demonic entity do to Paul? It buffeted him. "In 'A Critical Lexicon and Concordance to the English and New Testament', page 119, the word 'buffet' is translated, 'to strike with the hands, the fingers being clenched.'" [10]

That wasn't sickness, that was persecution. Everywhere Paul went as he preached the Gospel, people beat on him with their fists. It is very difficult to be proud when people are beating you with their fists, throwing rocks at you, putting you in prison and running you out of town.

Paul asked God three times to take the "thorn in the flesh", or persecution away from him, but God refused to do so, saying, "My grace is sufficient for thee: for my strength is made perfect in weakness." (2 Cor. 12:8)

The theologians pontificate on this by saying that Paul asked God three times to heal him and three times God told him, "No, my grace is sufficient for you to go through this sickness." But the Greek language used here does not in any way support that theory. Possibly this is where the idea came from that, "Sometimes God says 'No' when we ask Him to heal us," which is impossible because God has already said "Yes" in His Word that He **wants** us healed and in fact has already healed us.

Divine Healing Is Part Of The Atonement

"But he was wounded for our transgressions, he was bruised for our iniquities: the chastisement of our peace was upon him; and with his stripes we **are** healed." (Isa. 53:5) (author's emphasis)

"...Himself took our infirmities, and bare our sicknesses." (Matt. 8:17)

"Who his own self bare our sins in his own body on the tree, that we, being dead unto sins, should live unto righteousness: by whose stripes ye **were** healed." (1 Pet. 2:24) (author's emphasis) Notice that these scriptures do not say that "sometimes some Christians are healed." Divine healing is unconditionally connected to the Salvation which Jesus accomplished in the Atonement for the human race.

Isn't it strange that the theologians can accept the first part of the Atonement that says our sins have been paid for and all we have to do is come to Christ and receive forgiveness for those sins, but they reject the second part that just as clearly says that Jesus paid the price for the healing of our bodies and all we have to do is come to Christ and receive healing for our bodies?

Come to think of it, if it was really true that God sends sickness to teach His children some kind of lesson, then the only people who would be sick are Christians. Satan would not want to put sickness on people because he would only be helping God teach people those great lessons!

Finally, Paul said, "Therefore I take pleasure in *infirmities*, **(astheneia)** in reproaches, in necessities, in persecutions, in distresses for Christ's sake; for when I am weak, then am I strong." (2 Cor. 12:10) **He spells out in exact detail what the persecution was that he was referring to in this verse!**

Now Listen Carefully To This!

In the next chapter, Paul uses the same word, **astheneia**, when referring to the crucifixion of Christ. "For though he (Jesus) was crucified through *weakness*, **(astheneia)** ye he liveth by the power of God. For we also are weak in him, but we shall live with him by the power of God toward you." (2 Cor. 13:4)

It is as incorrect to say Paul gloried in his "sickness" as it is to say Jesus Christ was crucified through "sickness." *Yet the identical Greek Word is used in both verses!*

"Kakopatheia"—"The meaning is ill-plight, distress, suffer hardship, trouble other than sickness." [11]

"Is any among you *afflicted*? **(Kakopatheia)**...Is any *sick* **(astheneo)** among you?" (James 5:13,14)

"*Astheneo*" means weak, feeble, sick which clearly demonstrates the difference in this verse between *affliction* that is **persecution** and that which is a **physical sickness!** [12]

Finally, Paul gives a graphic picture of the persecution he was referring to in his writings.

"And what more shall I say? For the time would fail me to tell of Gideon, and of Barak, and of Samson, and of Jephthae; of David also, and Samuel, and of the prophets: who through faith subdued kingdoms, wrought righteousness, obtained promises, stopped the mouths of lions, quenched the violence of fire, escaped the edge of the sword, out of weakness were made strong, waxed valiant in fight, turned to flight the armies of the aliens. Women received their dead raised to life again: and others were tortured, not accepting deliverance; that they might obtain a better resurrection: and others had trial of cruel mockings and scourgings, yea, moreover of bonds and imprisonment: they were stoned, they were sawn asunder, were tempted, were slain with the sword: they wondered about in sheepskins and goatskins; being destitute, *afflicted*, **(thlibo)** tormented; (of whom the world was not worthy:) they wandered in deserts, and in mountains, and in dens and caves of the earth." (Heb. 11:32-38)

These are the situations and circumstances that God gives His children grace to go through victoriously toward the goal He has set before them!

The Martyr's Crown

What is the difference between dying a martyr's death and dying in a terrible accident or of a horrible disease? (1) Martyrs **choose** to die for their faith in Christ. They could recant and live, but the very idea is unthinkable because their faith and testimony in Christ is more important than life itself. (2) Martyrs receive a crown from God for their martydom which demonstrates the spiritual gain from such a choice and experience. (Rev. 2:10)

On the other hand, no mention is made of such a crown for those who die of diseases or accidents. It is true that they will go to Heaven if they have kept their faith in Christ for Salvation, but their death is usually premature and is not normally a faith-building experience. How many friends and relatives of the deceased have to fight a spirit of fear because Satan suggests that they, too, are going to die in the same manner? How many friends are angry at God for causing such suffering and for taking their loved one away from them? (*See "Strongman's His Name II ", pages 189-191, for further teaching concerning this fact*)

Christians will have troubles in this life, but they must be certain that the troubles aren't those they have the right to take authority over in the Name of Jesus and **stop.** The purpose of this book is to demonstrate from God's Word exactly what the tricks of Satan are and what the Truth is—what God does and what Satan does in our life. The simple truth is that sickness and accidents are not Godly actions so we should not be tricked by Satan and his demons into accept them, thinking they are something God wants us to experience for whatever reason. We have the authority of God's Word that we can pierce the deception of Satan with the Sword of the Spirit, which is the Word of God, and stand against the "wiles" of the enemy. (Eph. 6:11) We are more than conquerors through the Power of Jesus Christ! (Rom. 8:37) We don't have to put up with what sinners have to put up with because Jesus has given us 100% authority over Satan in His Name. (Luke 10:19) That is the Good News of the Gospel of Jesus Christ!

Jesus said, "In the world ye shall have tribulation: but be of good cheer; I have overcome the world." (John 16:33) The word "*tribulation*" is the word, "**thlipsis**", which means, according to Strong's Exhaustive Concordance of the Bible, word number 2347, "**anguish, burdened, persecution, trouble.**" The Zondervan Parallel New Testament in Greek and English, p. 325 uses the word, "**distress**".

The Christian's life will not be a bed of roses if he chooses to follow Christ. He will undoubtedly be persecuted for righteousness' sake. But the Good News of Jesus Christ is that He has overcome this world's system and the leader of that system, Satan. (Col. 2:15, Amplified Bible)

Now the child of God can draw upon that victory by distinguishing between what Satan would like to put on God's people and stop it by faith in God's Word, and face what God says His children must go through and receive His Strength and Wisdom to do so with power and joy!

A PRAYER OF FORGIVENESS

At this point I would like to lead you in a prayer of forgiveness if you have harbored anger and resentment toward God for the evil things that have taken place in your life. It is important to ask God to forgive you of those angry accusations to free yourself up to enter into the kind of loving relationship God desires to have with you. He understands the reason why you thought those things about Him. Just talk to Him as you would to the most loving person you have ever known.

Say, "Heavenly Father, I ask your forgiveness for harboring anger and resentment in my heart toward You for the terrible, evil things that have happened in my life. I see in your Word now that You aren't the One who does those things and that You actually want to protect me from the evil works of Satan if I will just believe and obey Your Word. Please forgive me for blaming You for what Satan was actually doing to me and my family.

"I thank you for forgiving me of my sins. Help me to draw closer to you and to trust you with every part of my life. I give myself completely to You because You are the best Friend I will ever have. I believe You will help me become all that You know I can be. I love you with all my heart, Heavenly Father. Amen."

"I rebuke you, Satan, for deceiving me about my Heavenly Father and from this point on I will resist you because I know what your evil works are now. I have repented of the anger and resentment I had in my heart toward God so you cannot use those open doors to harass me anymore. I am free from your bondage because the Word of God says, 'If the Son therefore shall make you free, ye shall be free indeed.'" (John 8:36)

"Thank you, Father God, for your freedom. I open my heart to Your Holy Spirit to lead me into all Truth so that I can be used of You to accomplish Your Will in my live. Amen."

CONCLUSION

As a result of the information you have read in this book, what kind of relationship should Christians have with their Heavenly Father when they understand God's Character, and secondarily, when they understand the character of Satan?

Since God is Love and His Love is Eternal, Christians will know that God truly loves them with a never failing love. He will never abuse them or do anything that is evil in their lives. He will seek to bring out the very best in them as they follow and obey His Word. They will understand that God is on their side—the best Friend they will ever have. He will never "throw them to the wolves" to see what they are made of, or to test their love for Him.

His method of teaching His children is through His Word, by His Holy Spirit. They understand that their Heavenly Father is the best thing that has ever happened to them and that it is an awesome privilege to be a child of God, with all the privileges that come with being a member of the Family of God. They also understand that just because God is Love does not signify that they can take advantage of that Love or get away with anything that is ungodly. They know He demands and expects obedience from His children, which is a further sign of His Love.

His discipline is not cruel or abusive, but firm and loving. However, those who continue on in disobedience will lose God's protection, which opens them to the fiery trials of the tormentor, Satan and his demons. Therefore, **God's children understand that it is intelligent to find out which way God is moving and then move with God.**

They will have a keen awareness of God's Holiness which brings an urgent desire to live a holy life because they know that Sin cost God the greatest Treasure of Heaven, His Only, Begotten Son, Jesus Christ. Therefore they reverence and respect Him for the fact that He will not tolerate sin in the lives of His children. They realize that sin kills and for that reason God wants to shield them from the ravaging effects of sin. They do not fear God as they would an abusive parent, but they give Him the holy, reverential honor that is due their Holy, Pure, Father God.

Because God and His Word do not change, Christians can have complete confidence that when they obey God's Word and meet His conditions, God will be absolutely faithful to do whatever He has promised in His Word. They know He is totally reliable so they can have unlimited, unwavering faith in God and His Word. They can trust Him with their lives because He will not take advantage of them in any part of their lives, and He will not desert them in their time of greatest need. Everything else in the Universe may fail, but God does not fail those who believe and receive by faith that which He has promised.

They understand that "luck" or "chance" have no part in their lives because God's Presence is continually upon them and He intensely desires to protect and care for His children's needs. Therefore, there is no reason to fear anything or anyone.

Jesus Demonstrates God The Father To Us

They are aware that Jesus is the perfect example of what their Father is. The revelation Jesus brought to the human race about His Father was and is the latest, up-to-date information that is available to mankind today. Through Jesus the Christian can get a graphic picture of what their Heavenly Father is like. The overwhelming evidence from the life of Jesus is that God is Good and does only good things. It is not within His Character to be evil or do anything that even hints of evil. Everything Jesus did on this earth was only good, so that is exactly what they can expect from their Heavenly Father also.

Since Jesus came to destroy Satan's tools of destruction, and in fact did that when He died and rose from the dead, they know that Satan cannot touch them if they stay away from sin and the works of the flesh and believe God's Promises. Satan is a defeated foe and it is their Father's Will for His children to keep Satan in a constant state of defeat in every part of their lives and in this world. They clearly understand that God will never initiate a satanic action in their lives for any reason because God's Will is for his children to experience the good things of God in their lives, such as: Salvation, eternal life, the Baptism or infilling of the Holy Spirit, good, physical health, happiness, peace, joy, needs supplied, liberty, and wisdom, which are but a few of the many blessings of God.

Christians know that there is nothing impossible with God. He is All-Powerful, All-Knowing and He is present everywhere at the same time by His Holy Spirit. Therefore, once God's Will is established in any given situation by what His Word and Holy Spirit say, the child of God can have complete confidence that God's Will shall be done in spite of what the circumstances may appear to be. God cannot fail and there is no righteous need that He will not provide when His children maintain their faith in Him and in His Word.

Interpretation Is Necessary

They know that the Old and New Testaments must be interpreted correctly if they are to receive the full measure of God's Word in their lives. The need for interpretation does not in any way, whatsoever, signify that certain parts of the Bible are not true or inspired. It only signifies that the revelation of God was not as clear in past dispensations as it has been since Jesus came to earth. Nor is it as clear at this time as it will be when God's people are in Heaven, in the very presence of God, as God continues to reveal Himself throughout the endless ages of Eternity.

The believer understands that God's Character, as revealed in the Bible, is to be the measuring stick for deciding whether those actions attributed to God are truly Godly, or whether in actuality they are of Satan, the great deceiver.

The child of God understands that the Justice of God demands punishment for each and every sin that has ever been committed. For that reason there are many occasions in the Old Testament when it appeared that God was operating our-of-control when He dealt with sin and the resulting judgment which followed. But the Law was mankind's schoolmaster to teach them the fact that sin is an unthinkable act. The anger and wrath that was caused in a Righteous God was a visual example of how deadly and terrible the consequences of sin are so that mankind could grasp the significance of how horrible and evil sin is.

Through God's Grace and Mercy, Jesus came to earth to satisfy God's Justice by dying, as the Perfect Sacrifice for Sin, in the place of every member of the human race. His shed blood satisfied God's Justice for every sin the human race has ever committed. Now, by accepting Christ as their Lord and Savior and by receiving the forgiveness of their sins by faith in God's Word, they receive Eternal Life instead of death which they deserve.

Christians know Satan's desire is to keep this tremendous, earthshaking truth from reaching the human race. Through his continual deception he attempts to obscure God's answer for sin. He tricks mankind into breaking God's Moral Laws that are meant to not only maintain order on the earth, but to also point the human race to the only remedy for their sinful condition, the Lamb, Christ Jesus.

What Satan Wants Is Not What He Gets

God's children know that they have total power over Satan in the Name of Satan's Conqueror, Jesus Christ. They have been given the right to use that power to accomplish

God's Will on this earth, which is to reach every living soul with the Good News of the Gospel of Jesus Christ. Satan is the outlaw/vigilante, who operates outside the Law, so it is the responsibility of the child of God to "arrest" him in the Name of Jesus, and keep him in such a bound, dominated state that he is not at liberty to do what he would like to do in the human race. Only after the body of believers, who are looking for Jesus to return for them, are taken out of this earth to Heaven will Satan have the freedom to operate as he desires. But that will be for a very short season.

They understand that God is the Judge of all mankind. As such, He cannot be held morally guilty for His actions in judging those depraved nations and people who flagrantly disobey His Moral Laws, anymore than a judge today is guilty of murder when he sentences a murderer to be executed for his crimes. In operating as an arm of the Law, God is only completing His duty to honor His just Laws that were set in motion for the good of all mankind.

Nor were the Israelites guilty of murder when they acted as a national executioner of those nations who had been sentenced to receive the results of the Law of sin and death in their lives. In the Age of Grace that we live in today, the judgment of God for sins will not come until the end of this dispensation. What people receive for their sins now are the wages of sin.

God's people know that God is not the author of Sin, evil, Satan and his demons, of wars, sickness, misery, abortions, murder, accidents, calamities, acts of Nature, poverty, or any other wicked kind of behavior. They do not believe those who seek to assassinate the Character of God by blaming Him for such things. They put the blame for those evil things where they belong—**on the pathological liar, homicidal killer and universal pervert, Satan.**

As a result of this knowledge, Christians are freed from the conflicting, confusing, destructive deception of Satan to enter into a beautiful, healthy, loving relationship with their Heavenly Father which enables them to live a rich, satisfying life as children of the Most High God while, at the same time, seeking to become all that God envisioned they would be from before the time the foundations of this world were established!

How thankful we can be that we have such a wonderful, magnificent Heavenly Father.

Proper Interpretation Requires Discipline

Now, use these basic tools to rightly divide/ interprete those "problem" scriptures that you encounter in the Bible. It is not possible to cover each and every incident here, so it will require that you search the scriptures and arrive at the Truth of God's Word for yourself. These may not be all the rules of interpretation, but they will be what is needed to establish God's true Character.

1. What is the context ? Is there agreement in context between the scriptures under consideration?

2. Where is the weight of Scripture on the subject? What does the entire Bible say about the matter?

3. What did Jesus have to say about it? If a scripture does not agree with what Jesus said about the subject something is out of sync.

4. Establish first in your heart what God's Character is. Then judge Scripture by God's Character as revealed in the Bible, not God's Character by what a certain scripture may appear to say.

5. Use the New Testament to interpret the Old Testament. We live in the dispensation of Grace today, not under the Law. When in doubt, lean toward the New Testament application of Truth in your interpretation.

6. If there is any conflict between the Old and the New Testament, a mistake has been made in interpretation which must be corrected by using the above rules.

APPENDIX I

THE 74 CHARGES JOB MADE AGAINST GOD

"1. The Lord taketh away (1:22), Satan did this (1:6-19)

2. What?...shall we not receive evil? (2:10). God cannot tempt men with evil (James 1:13-16). We are to pray 'deliver us from evil'—not deliver us from God (Mat. 6:13)

3. God has hedged in-with calamity

4. The arrows of the Almighty are within me, the poison thereof drinks up my spirit (6:4)

5. The terrors of God do set themselves in array against me

6. God scares me with dreams, and terrifies me through visions; so that my soul chooses strangling and death rather than life (7:14)

7. You have set me as a mark against You (7:20)

8. You do not pardon my transgressions

9. He (God) breaks me with tempest (9:17)

10. He multiplies my wounds without cause

11. He will not suffer me to take my breath (9:18)

12. He fills me with bitterness

13. He destroys the perfect with the wicked (9:22)

14. He will laugh at the trial of the innocent (9:23)

15. He has given the earth to the wicked

16. He hides the face of the judges so that they cannot discern right and wrong

17. If I made myself ever so clean, yet You will plunge me into the ditch (9:30,31)

18. You oppress and despise me (10:3)

19. You shine upon the counsel of the wicked

20. You know that I am not wicked, yet You destroy me (10:7-8)

21. You have poured me out like milk, and curdled me like cheese (10:10)

22. If I sin, then You mark me and will not forgive me (10:14)

23. You hunt me as a fierce lion (10:16)

24. You renew Your witness against me, and increase wrath upon me (10:17)

25. The tabernacles of robbers prosper, and they that provoke God are secure; into whose hand God brings abundance (12:6)

26. Though He slay me, yet will I trust Him (13:15)

27. You hide Your face from me and count me as Your enemy (13:24)

28. You write bitter things against me, and make me possess the iniquities of my youth (13:26)

29. You put my feet in stocks (13:27)

30. You destroy the hope of man (14:19)

31. He has made me weary (16:70)

32. Made desolate all my company

33: Filled me with wrinkles (16:8)

34. He tears me in wrath (16:9)

35. Hates me

36. Gnashes upon me with His teeth

37. Has delivered me to the ungodly, into the hands of the wicked 16:11)

38. Has broken me asunder (16:12)

39. Has taken me by the neck and shaken me to pieces

40. Has set me up for his mark

41. His archers compassed me (16:13)

42. He cleaves my reins

43. He does not spare me

44. He pours out my gall upon the ground

45. Breaks me with breach upon breach (16:14)

46. Runs upon me like a giant

47. He has done all this for no injustice in my hands (16:7)

48. He has made me a byword of the people (17:6)

49. God has overthrown me (19:6)

50. Compassed me in His net

51. He does not hear me (19:7)

52. There is no justice from Him (19:7)

53. He has fenced up my way that I cannot pass (19:8)

54. He has set darkness in my paths

55. Stripped me of my glory (19:9)

56. Taken my crown

57. Destroyed me on every side (19:10)

58. Removed my hope like a tree

59. Kindled His wrath against me (19:11)

60. Counted me as one of His enemies

61. His troops raise up their way against me, and encamp round my house (19:12)

62 He has put my brethren far from me

63. Estranged my acquaintances (19:13)

64. The almighty troubles me (23:16)

65. God has taken away my judgment (27:2)

66. Vexed my soul

67. Loosed my cord (30:11)

68. Afflicted me

69. Cast me into the mire (30:19)

70. I cry to You, and You do not hear me (30:20)

71. I stand up and You do not regard me

72. You are become cruel to me (30:21)

73. You oppose me

74. You have lifted me up to the wind and have dissolved my substance (30:22)

"All the above 74 statements are untrue, for it was Satan who took away his substance (1:12-19), terrorized him, and did all the other cruel things to Job (2:6-7; 42:10). At first Job did not sin with his lips or charge God foolishly, but after his friends came and he endured long months of suffering, he began to sin thus. For this he repented (40:1-6; 42:1-6)"[1]

Notice in Job 1:11 and 2:5 that Satan suggested first of all that God bring destruction upon Job and his possessions. But God refused to do so because He is not the destroyer. If there was to be any destruction, it was Satan who would do it.

The only reason Satan had any right whatsoever to even suggest that Job deserved what he had in mind for him was because Job had allowed an open door or loophole of opportunity in his life through fear. "For the thing which I greatly feared is come upon me, and that which I was afraid of is come unto me." (3:25)

A **great** fear is no small thing in spiritual matters. 2 Timothy 1:7 informs the reader that fear is a demonic spirit. "For God hath not give us the spirit of fear; but of power, and of love, and of a sound mind." Fear is actually believing what Satan has to say about the situation, which is directly opposed to God's Word. Fear is a sin, and sin opens people up to Satan's attention, deception, and intervention in their lives. This is how people, "...give place to the devil" which Paul talks about in Ephesians 4:27. Job had given Satan a place, or toehold, or loophole through fear, which Satan then exploited.

Listen to Satan Whine

Satan's complaint to God was that God was still protecting Job with a hedge around him and his possessions when Job really deserved to be worked over satanicly because of the open door to fear. Only Satan would have the gall to demand his "rights" from God when he is the most wretched outlaw in the Universe who breaks every law there is. But God is even fair with the devil.

God's Mercy can be seen in the situation because He limited what Satan could do to Job despite the fact that Job had opened himself up to satanic action because of his sin. God's Mercy still protects even sinners to a certain extent, because if He did not, Satan would kill every sinner in an instant—he is that evil, cruel and without mercy or conscience. This is why it is best to throw ourselves on the Mercy of God when we sin, because that decision and resulting action on God's part places us outside the range of the merciless onslaughts of Satan.

ISN'T GOD GOOD? YES HE IS—ALL THE TIME!

APPENDIX 2

By permission of Johnny Hart
and Creators Syndicate, Inc.

BIBLIOGRAPHY

Chapter One

1. Perry, Jack. "Did God Kill My Baby?" Voice Magazine. Vol. 36. Feb., 1988. ps. 10-14.

2. Farah, Joseph. Editor "Between the Lines." Why Ted Turner Hates Christianity." AFA Journal. July, 1990. ps. 12,13.

3. Newsweek. Aug. 15, 1988, p. 47.

Chapter Two

1. " $16 Million Lotter Jackpot Becomes Winner's Nightmare." Statesman Journal. Salem, OR. Aug. 29, 1996. p. 8A.

2. Jayne, Greg. "UO Coach Finds Solace On Field." Statesman Journal. Salem, OR. Oct. 2, 1993. p. 5A.

3. Van Buren, Abigail. "Special Boarding Schools Available." The Sunday Oregonian. Portland, OR. Nov. 27, 1988.

4. Willing, Richard and Peter Eisler. "Modern Age Powerless Next To 'Act of God.' USA Today Newspaper. Jan. 9, 1996. p. 1A.

5. Edmonds, Patricia. "18% Call Floods Retribution. "USA Today Newspaper. July 23, 1993. p. 1A.

6. "Indians Call Devastating Quake God's Will." Statesman Journal. Salem, OR. Oct. 2, 1993. p. 5A.
7. "Day Of Doom Passes Without Quake." Statesman Journal. May 4, 1993. p. 6C.

8. "Poll Finds More Americans See God As Judge Than Forgiver." Pentecostal Evangel. Feb. 6, 1994. p.15.

9. "AIDS Survey. "USA Today Newspaper. Mar. 27, 1996. p. 1D.

10. Schurch, Maylan. Signs of the Times. July, 1992. p. 13. Excerpt from book, "Rescue From Beyond Orion." 1987. Pacific Press.

11. Dake, Finis Jennings. (1963) Dakes Annotated Reference Bible. Dake Bible Sales, Inc. note "m", Heb. 1:3.

12. Wooding, Dan. "God's Wake-Up Call?" Charisma Magazine. July, 1994. p.26.

13. Hoberg, Rev. Ed. Private conversation.

Chapter Three

1. Dake, Finis Jennings. (1963) Dakes Annotated Reference Bible. Dake Bible Sales, Inc., note "d", Matt. 5:17.

2. Ibid. letter "c", Heb. 8:13.

3. Carlson, G. Raymond. (1975) Preparing To Teach God's Word. Gospel Publishing House. p. 72.

4. Hoberg, Ed. private conversation.

5. Dake, Finis Jennings. (1963) Dakes Annotated Reference Bible. Dake Bible Sales, Inc., note "q", Matt. 6:13.

6. Copeland, Kenneth. "Questions And Answers. "Believer's Voice of Victory.Jan. 1995. p. 23.

7. Ibid. p. 23.

8. Robeson, Carol and Robeson, Jerry. (1983) Strongman's His Name What's His Game. Shiloh Publishing House. p. 53.

9. Cornwall, Judson. "The Man Who Really Knew God." Charisma Magazine. Jan. 1987. p. 29.

Chapter Four

1. Garlow, Jim. "Jesus The Fulfillment Of The Covenant." Christ for the Nations. Dec. 1990. p. 3.

2. Ibid. p. 3.

3. Gallaher, William. "Knowing God's Character." People's Church. Sermon taken from audio tape, Salem, OR. Jan. 14, 1996.

4. Rosio, Robert. (1994) Satanization of Society. Prescott Press, Inc. p. 88.

5. Gill, John. (1978) Complete Body of Doctrinal and Practical Divinity. Vol. 1. Baker Book House. p. 46.

6. Pink, Arthur W. (1975) Gleanings in the Godhead. Moody Press. ps. 31.

7. Thiessen, Henry Clarence. (1949) Lectures in Systematic Theology. revised by Vernon D. Doerksen. William B. Eerdmans Publishing Co. p. 82.

8. Shedd, W.G.T. Dogmatic Theology. Vol. 1. p. 384.

9. Pink, Arthur W. (1975) Gleanings in the Godhead. Moody Press. p. 20.

10. Spittler, Russell P. God the Father. Undated Teacher's Manual. Gospel Publishing House. p. 65.
11. Ibid. p. 61.

12. Pink, Arthur W. (1975) Gleanings in the Godhead. Moody Press. ps. 35.

13. Dake, Finis Jennings. (1963) Dakes Annotated Reference Bible. Dake Bible Sales, Inc., note "m", Heb. 1:3.

14. Spittler, Russell P. God the Father. Undated Teacher's Manual. Gospel Publishing House. p. 71.

15. Brunner, Emil. The Christian Doctrine of God. Dogmatics V. 1. English Trans Olive Wyon, Lutterworth Press 1949. The Westminster Press. no date. p. 163.

Chapter Five

1. Williams, Ernest S. (1953) Systematic Theology. Vol. 1. Gospel Publishing House. p. 189.

2. Thiessen, Henry Clarence. (1949) Lectures in Systematic Theology. revised by Vernon D. Doerksen. William B. Eerdmans Publishing Co. p.85.

3. Gill, John. (1978) Complete Body of Doctrinal and Practical Divinity. Vol. 1. Baker Book House. ps. 156,157.

4. Time Magazine, 1974. p. 59.

5. Wilkerson, David. "The Pain of God." Times Square Church Pulpit Series. June 5, 1995. ps. 2,3.

6. Franz, Norman N. "Is God Judging America." Unravelling the New World Order. June, 1995. ps. 1,3,4.

7. Stamps, Donald C. (1990) The Full Life Study Bible-New Testament. Zondervan Bible Publishers. p. 336.

8. Dake, Finis Jennings, (1963) Dake's Annotated Reference Bible. Dake Bible Sales, Inc., note "a", Judges 16:28.

9. Ibid. note "d", 2 Chron. 20:22.

Chapter Six

1. Pink, Arthur W. (1975) Gleanings in the Godhead. Moody Press. p. 55.

2. Gill, John. (1978) Complete Body of Doctrinal and Practical Divinity. Vol. 1. Baker Book House. p. 133.

3. Hinn, Benny. "Do You Believe In Miracles?" This Is Your Day For A Miracle. Fall, 1995. p. 4.

4. Ibid. p. 4.

5. Ibid. p. 4.

6. Spittler, Russell P. God the Father. Undated Teacher's Manual. Gospel Publishing House. p. 79.

7. Charnock, Stephen. (1958) The Existence and Attributes of God. Photolithoprinted by Cushing-Malloy, Inc. ps. 764,764.

8. Pink, Arthur W. (1975) Gleanings in the Godhead. Moody Press. p. 60.

9. Finney, Charles G. "No More Excuses." Decision Magazine. Dec. 1994. p. 34. Taken from "On Trusting the Mercy of God," in "Sermons on Gospel Themes." 1876 B.J. Goodrich. Fleming H. Revell Co. Baker Book House Co.

10. Wilkerson, David. "God Won't Walk Out On You!" Times Square Church Pulpit Series. Oct. 9, 1995. p. 1.

11. Pink, Arthur W. (1975) Gleanings in the Godhead. Moody Press. p. 126.

12. Williams, Ernest S. (1953) Systematic Theology. Vol. 1. Gospel Publishing House. p. 197.

13. Gerrish, Jim. "Faithfulness." Jerusalem Prayer Letter. July, 1995. p. 1.

14. Ibid. p. 1.

15. Wilkerson, David. "Father's Love." Times Square

Church Pulpit Series. Jan.17, 1994. p. 3.

16. Pink, Arthur W. (1975) Gleanings in the Godhead. Moody Press. p. 51.

17. Spittler, Russell P. God the Father. Undated Teacher's Manual. Gospel Publishing House. p. 87,88.

18. Pink, Arthur W. (1975) Gleanings in the Godhead. Moody Press. p. 77,78.

19. Wilkerson, David. "The Pain of God." TImes Square Church Pulpit Series. June 5, 1995. ps. 2,3.

Chapter Seven

Chapter Eight

1. Name withheld. "Flowers Weren't Enough." Decision Magazine. April, 1995. p. 33.

2. Dake, Finis Jennings. (1963) Dakes Annotated Reference Bible. Dake Bible Sales, Inc., note "u", 1 Pet. 4:16.

3. Wilkerson, David. "The Persecution Of The Righteous." Times Square Church Pulpit Series. April 13, 1987. p. 2.

4. Dake, Finis Jennings. (1963) Dakes Annotated Reference Bible. Dake Bible Sales, Inc., note "h", 2 Cor. 1:4.

5. Ibid. note "k", 2 Cor. 1:6.

6. Ibid. note "i", 2 Cor. 1:5-7.

7. Ibid. note "d", Heb. 11:25.

8. Ibid. note "i", 2 Cor. 12:10.

9. Ibid. note "h"2 Cor. 12:7.

10. Robeson, Carol and Robeson, Jerry. (1983) Strongman's His Name What's His Game. Shiloh Publishing House. p. 98.

11. Dake, Finis Jennings. (1963) Dake's Annotated Reference Bible. Dake Bible Sales, Inc., note "c", James 5:13.

12. Ibid. note "d", James 5:14.

Conclusion

Appendix I

1. Dake, Finis Jennings. (1963) Dake's Annotated Reference Bible. Dake Bible Sales, Inc., note "e", Job 1:22.

Appendix 2

1. Used by permission of Johnny Hart and Creators Syndicate, Inc.

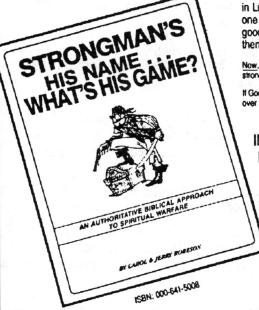

Mighty Warriors Junior

Activity & Coloring Book
Price: $8.95

Life can be so much easier if we learn the basics of correct spiritual warfare while still a child. These basic principles are taught in an interesting positive approach. Even children can learn about being an overcomer and more than a conqueror. More than ever before we need to teach children how to stop the devil's influence in their lives. They will learn about putting on the whole armor of God, using their shield of faith, etc. while they are going through this beautiful 96 page book of activities and things to color. The book is designed for ages 6-13. We give unlimited rights with each book to teachers or parents to make photocopies for their own use in the classroom or home schooling.

Riding in the Chariot to Victory

Introduction to Spiritual Warfare

...a powerful guide to victory over satan and the forces of darkness.

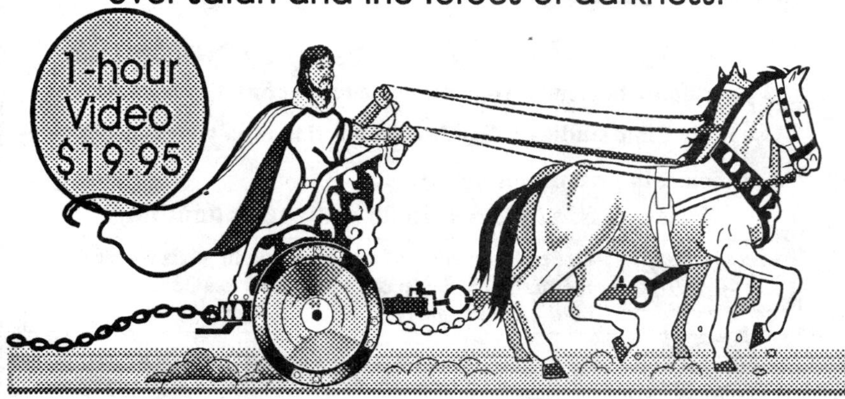

Never again do we have to be intimidated by the deceptions of the devil. He is powerless if we keep him in the arena of God's Word. Don't listen to his lies and fears...they are the only weapons he has left. God took the devil's weapons and Jesus destroyed them. Now we are more than conquerers through Christ. We are with Christ in the chariot...the devil is bound, chained to the back of the chariot where he will remain if we believe what God says.

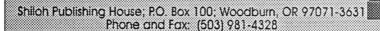

Shiloh Publishing House; P.O. Box 100; Woodburn, OR 97071-3631
Phone and Fax: (503) 981-4328

SUDDENLY... ONE WAS TAKEN!

by Dr. Jerry Robeson

INTERESTED IN WHAT IS GOING TO TAKE PLACE IN THE NEAR FUTURE?

You will want to read this action packed adventure of the Great Tribulation story in light of the Bible Prophecy, Scientific advances, the New Age and world events. Steve's wife is instantly raptured leaving him to face life under the antichrist, false prophet and the image of the beast.

The highlight of the book is the dramatic, emotion-laced Second Coming of Jesus Christ to earth, with multitudes of Christians and angels, to establish His Kingdom.

Dr. Jerry Robeson, Ph.D.

$10.95 plus s/h
ISBN # 000-146-8685

SHILOH PUBLISHING HOUSE BOOK & TAPE CATALOG

SPIRITUAL WARFARE

STRONGMAN'S HIS NAME ...WHAT'S HIS GAME? BOOK

Instead of binding just symptoms we stop in Jesus' Name the sixteen strong-men or demonic spirits mentioned by name in the Bible. Contains diagrams in tree form illustrating each strongman. Tells how and what to bind and loose in each situation.

8 ½ " X 11", 163 page paperback.

Price: $13.95

Strongman's His Name II

You'll want this if you liked the first book. Sequel to the Robeson's original book answers over 150 of the most asked questions regarding spiritual warfare plus explanations of many new topics. Some of the questions answered are: Why do I seem to have so much trouble with the devil if he's defeated?, What was the curse put on all Viet Nam soldiers?, Can Satan read our minds? 5½" X 8½", 228 page paperback.

Price: $13.95

TRUST GOD
He Really Does Love You

Dr. Jerry Robeson's newest book is a winner! Scripturally balanced character analysis of God the Father—what He does and does not do. Exposes traditions of men. Explains God's misunderstood actions in O.T. & difference between Godly discipline & devilish abuse. Enlarges faith in God. 6'X9" paper. $10.95

Six-Cassette Strongman Series With Booklet

Listen to the Strongman I **book-on-tape** while driving or working. Narrated by Jerry and Carol Robeson. Price: $29.95

Three-Ring Notebook with 6 cassettes and the Strongman book

Combines the **complete book**, together with the Strongman I **book-on-tape** in a beautiful binder. For the serious Bible student or teacher. Price: $39.95

Delux 12-Cassette Series

Set contains Strongman I **book-on-tape**, Gifts of the Holy Spirit Series, Victory Over Fear Series and two booklets. Price: $49.95

8-Hour Strongman Video Tape Seminar

Recorded in front of a "live" audience. Just like being in the seminar in person! An excellent tool for classes & Bible studies.

Price: $149.95

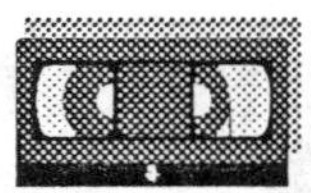

1-Hour Video, *"Riding In The Chariot To Victory!"*

Dr. Jerry Robeson shows how the devil is disarmed, defeated & disgraced & that we have total victory over him in the Name of Jesus. We ride in the chriot with Jesus & the devil is chained to the back of the chariot. We are more than conquerors through Christ Jesus.

Price: $19.95

6-Hour Live Seminar on four audio cassettes

Jerry and Carol teach a city-wide seminar. This set captures the feel of actually being there in person.

Price: $20.00

Laminated Reference Card

Lists the 16 trongmen, their symptoms, the vorks of the flesh and some of ne most important scriptures for oing spiritual warfare effec-ively. **Just the right size to arry in your Bible** 5½"X8½". Price: $3.00

BOOKS

Spanish Strongman Book, *La Guerra Espiritual*"

The Spanish text is the same as English but the format is smaller nd comes without the side nargins for notes. 5½" X 8½", 22 pg. paperback.
Price: $10.95

Strongman Booklet

A bare-bones, 40-page ooklet with the tree diagrams nd a brief explanation of each strongman. Recommend purchase of complete book first.
Price: $4.00

Faith In Eruption

Read Jerry Robeson's account about the tremendous revival in Managua, Nicaragua as people were healed, delivered, raised from the dead and how a country was stirred by God just before an earthquake destroyed the city. Nicaragua had its Jonah! Price: $1.00

Suddenly...One Was Taken!

Jerry Robeson. A novel of spine-tingling suspense that climaxes with the glorious, triumphant Second Coming of Jesus Christ. Steve Adam's wife is caught away in the rapture, leaving Steve alone to face the horrible events of the Great Tribulation. 213 Pages
Price: $10.95

Mighty Warriors Jr. Activity & Coloring Book

Learning spiritual warfare on a child's level is made easy and positive! Many people have told us their life would have been so much better if they could have learned correct spiritual warfare principles while they were still children. 96 fun-packed pages that can be photocopied to use in the church classroom or private schooling.
Price: $8.95

MUSIC CASSETTES

All In The Name Of Jesus.

Smooth trumpet music and singing by Jerry Robeson playing favorites of the Church. *He's Everything to Me, Jesus Is All The World, All In The Name of Jesus, Surely the Presence, Rise aand Be Healed, All My Life, Reach Out to Jesus, Medley, I am Unworthy and Jesus Is Coming Soon.* Price: $6.00

In The Valley He Restoreth My Soul

The golden, mellow trumpet and singing of Jerry Robeson. *In The Valley He Restoreth My Soul, Wouldn't Take Nothing For My Journey Now, He Touched Me, I'm On The Battlefield, How Can You Live Without Him, Unworthy, When They Ring Those Golden Bells, Lovest Thou Me, I Am A Pilgrim, How Great Thou Art, His Grace Is Sufficient For Me and Children of the Lord.* Price: $6.00

Solid Gold Trumpet.

A cassette loaded with Jerry's royal trumpet sound playing the golden oldies and a few newer 14 kt. nuggets! All ones you'll enjoy listening to over and over again. *Because He Lives, He Touched Me, What A Friend, Old Rugged Cross, When the Saints Go Marching In, At The Cross, I Just Feel Like Something Good Is About To Happen!, Softy and Tenderly, Amazing Grace.* Price: $6.00

SINGLE CASSETTES

Verses of Praise From Psalms

Dr. Carol Robeson reads 30 minutes of Psalms chosen carefully to lift you up in praise to the Lord. Price: $2.00

Can Satan Understand Tongues or Read Your Mind?

Two of the most commonly misunderstood questions that people are afraid to ask or even think. Carol shows the truth scripturally on both subjects.
Price: $4.00

Conquering the Giants of Your Life.

Do you keep meeting obstacles in your Christian life? You can be the conquerer over all the giants of your life. Don't live in the valley of defeat another day. Learn to win both the battles and the war. Price: $4.00

SINGLE CASSETTES

God's Royal Road To Success

You can know the secrets to spiritual success and attainment by using simple biblical principles. Exchange old habits and life styles. Conquer fears and move into the abundant life Christ promised you! Price: $4.00

How To Receive Your Prayer Language

Join Carol as she teaches about the Holy Spirit in prophecy, outpouring and promise. Then in two easy half-steps learn how to receive and begin speaking fluently in your very own prayer language. Price: $4.00

Rise and Be Healed!

Healing is for you today. Jerry and Carol have seen thousands healed in their ministry. Carol now teaches you how to successfully ask, seek and recceive from God. Price: $4.00

Run To Win!

Spectators don't win races. Carol challenges you to be a success in life. Learn the Bible way to set and achieve your goals. Price:$4.00

What's Wrong With Rock Music?

Do young people around you need teaching about their music? Suzanne Saks uses her radio/ television degree knowledge to show Rock and Roll dangers from a young person's perspective. Price: $4.00

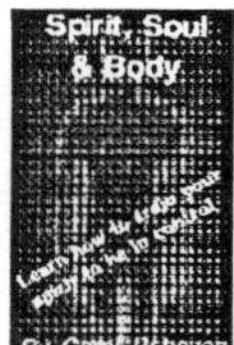

Spirit, Soul & Body

Hebrews says that only the sword of the Word can divide between spirit and soul. God's Word will help your understanding of this subject and put your spirit in control under the authority of the Holy Spirit. Understanding this will bring you crucial growth in your life. Price: $4.00

The Holy Spirit In Esther

Esther was an annointed lady. She was groomed by the Holy Spirit just like He wants to do for you. You can discover the same leadership qualitites in you that made Esther God's chosen vessel. Price: $4.00

The Mystery Of Job

What happened to Job? Was he used as a ping-pong ball between God and Satan? Can this happen to us? The Bible shows him as a double-minded man who invited disaster. *"The thing I greatly feared has come upon me."* Fear opens us to the hassles of the enemy. Carol brings balance to the book of Job. Price: $4.00

False Prophecy Unmasked

Carol teaches how to recognize areas of false visions and utterances. How to know what is for real and what is the deadly deception of familiar spirits speaking. See how clearly scripture reveals the difference. Price: $4.00

2-CASSETTE SERIES

Victory Over Fear!

Jerry teach[es] about the spirit [of] this age that seeks [to] rob and neutrali[ze] Christians of their spiritual vita[l]ity. Learn how to walk free [in] love, power and have a sou[nd] mind. Discover how you can [be] more than a conquerer. You [will] never feel like a 98 pound spiritual weakling again! Pric[e:] $8.00

Good Things Come From God!

Jerr[y] teaches us th[at] God is not a temperamental og[re] but a loving, heavenly Fath[er] that we can have confidence i[n]. He is the best friend we hav[e]. Once we learn who God is an[d] what He really does we wi[ll] never be confused about Hi[m] again. Price: $8.00

4-CASSETTE ALBUMS

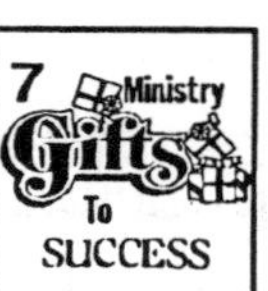

Seven Ministry Gifts to Success

God gave each of us spe[-]cial ministry gifts when we wer[e] born-again according to Roman[s] 12. Do you know what your[s] are? Carol points you to cleare[r] understanding of yourself a[s] well as those around you. Lear[n] how to develop your outstanding, God-given abilities to bles[s] your family and the whole bod[y] of Christ. Price: $15.00

4-CASSETTE ALBUMS

The 9 Gifts of the Holy Spirit

The Holy Spirit has ·laced His gifts in the Body of :hrist for the edification of the ·hole Church. He wants you, he layman as well as the minis- :r to understand and be filled ·ith His annointing power for ·reater service. Did you know hat as a born-again child of God ·ou already possess the poten- ·al for all nine of these Gifts to ·perate through you? Study ·ith Carol and find out how to elease His omnipotent power. 'our cassettes plus study guide. 'rice: $15.00

The Fruit of the Spirit

The fruit of the Spirit are to be planted, watered, weeded and tended to on a regular basis in order to reap a harvest. This **four cassette series** helps you see the importance of fruit-bearing in your life. The fruit you bear now will last for eternity. Price: $15.00

Shiloh means, a place of peace and prosperity. We pray that when you purchase our materials, you will receive blessings in abundance from the only giver of peace on this earth, our Lord Jesus Christ!

12-CASSETTE ALBUM

Delux Gifts Set

The delux gift set is composed of **three 4-cassette series:** The Nine Gifts of the Spirit, The Seven Ministry Gifts to Success and the Fruit of the Spirit plus one booklet on the Nine Gifts of the Spirit. Price: $39.95

Postage Charges on Orders

Up to $4	$1.30
$5 to $16.95	$2.15
$17 to $29.95	$2.65
$30 to $49.95	$3.25
$50 to $100	$4.50
$101 to $150	$5.00
Over $150	$5.00 plus add $1.00 per each additional $50 in merchandise.

U.P.S., Canada & Foreign, extra

Payment in U.S. dollars must accompany order. Please include postage.
Thank you! Make all Checks payable to: Shiloh Publishing House.
P.O. Box 100; Woodburn, OR 97071-3631; USA
1-800-607-6195

Title or Description	Qty	Price/Each	Total

Name: ______________________ **Subtotal:** __________

Address: ______________________ **Postage/H:** __________

City: __________ **State:** ___ **Zip:** __________ **TOTAL:** __________

VISA _____ **MC** _____ **Exp. date:** __________

Card #: ______________________

Signature: ______________________

About the Robesons

Dr. Jerry and Dr. Carol Robeson were Assembly of God missionari to Latin America for 20 years. They ministered in Nicaragua, Costa Ric Paraguay, Jamaica, Mexico and Chile. They specialized in open-air crusad which were held every night in an area of the city where a new church w needed. One crusade church in Costa Rica, for example, has more than 500 people in attendance and is constructing a building that seats 8000 people

The Robesons have also maintained an active television and radi ministry. They have produced and directed more than 700 Christia television programs in Latin America and the U.S. and many hundreds radio broadcasts. They have appeared in the U.S. on the Trinity Broadcastin Network PTL programs in Seattle, WA, Portland, OR, Phoenix, AZ, Saginav MI, and Miami, FL, the "Joy" program, the "California Tonight" progra on Channel 42 in Concord, CA and the "Good Life" program on Channel 2 in Clearwater, FL and affiliate stations. They regularly host the "Northwe Praise the Lord" program in Portland, OR each month.

Jerry and Carol are graduates of Northwest College of the Assemblie of God, Kirkland, WA, where Jerry earned a B.A. degree and Carol earne an A.A. degree. On May 31, 1981 Jerry received membership in the Delt Epsilon Chi Honor Society from the Northwest College in Kirkland, WA fo recognition of outstanding achievement. Both Jerry and Carol received Ph.D. in Theology on June 23, 1996 from Vision International University.

Jerry is the author of three books, *"Faith In Eruption,"* and *"I'r Healed...Put the Coffin Back,"* and *"Suddenly...One Was Taken!"* Jerry is als a soloist trumpeter on a number of long-playing albums. The *"Suddenly...On Was Taken!"* book has been translated into Danish by a publishing house i Denmark and is being distributed in 18 countries of Europe.

Carol has authored, *God's Royal Road*, and a children's book entitle *"Mighty Warriors Jr., Activity and Coloring Book."* She has also produced a fu line of visualized children's stories.

Jerry and Carol have co-authored their book, *"Strongman's Hi Name...What's His Game?"* Since the book's release it has been receive enthusiastically by those who are looking for sound, biblical instruction o spiritual warfare which in turn has triggered their seminar ministry. Th book is now in Spanish and is being distributed in the U.S. and Latin Americ The sequel to Strongman, *"Strongman's His Name II,"* was released in 1994 Both Strongman books have recently translated into Korean and are bein distributed world-wide by a publishing house in Seoul, Korea.

Although the Robesons are no longer appointed missionaries the still minister periodically in crusades and seminars throughout the world They also maintain The Life Center in Vilsonville, OR, where people ca come and hear the Word of God or attend their 4-year Bible College.

Life Vision Bible College & Seminary offers course that can be take either at one of the local campuses or by correspondence.

The Robesons periodically put out a free newsletter with articles about spiritual warfare. If you would like to be on their mailing list, please type or print your name and address clearly and send it to: Shiloh Publishing House, P.O. Box 100, Woodburn, OR 97071.